PLANET BROADBAND

Rouzbeh Yassini, Ph.D.

Cisco Press

800 East 96th Street, 3rd Floor
Indianapolis, Indiana 46240 USA

Planet Broadband

Rouzbeh Yassini, Ph.D.

Contributions from Stewart Schley, Leslie Ellis, and Roger Brown

Published by:
Cisco Press
800 East 96th Street, 3rd Floor
Indianapolis, Indiana 46240 USA

ISBN: 1-58720-090-2

Library of Congress Cataloging-in-Publication Number: 2003104988

Printed in the United States of America   1 2 3 4 5 6 7 8 9 0

First Printing   September 2003

Warning and Disclaimer

Trademark Acknowledgments

Feedback Information

At Cisco Press, our goal is to create in-depth technical books of the highest quality and value. Each book is crafted with care and precision, undergoing rigorous development that involves the unique expertise of members from the professional technical community.

Readers' feedback is a natural continuation of this process. If you have any comments regarding how we could improve the quality of this book, or otherwise alter it to better suit your needs, you can contact us through e-mail at feedback@ciscopress.com. Please make sure to include the book title and ISBN in your message.

We greatly appreciate your assistance.

Publisher	**John Wait**
Editor-In-Chief	**John Kane**
Executive Editor	**Jim Schachterle**
Cisco Representative	**Anthony Wolfenden**
Cisco Press Program Manager	**Sonia Torres Chavez**
Cisco Marketing Communications Manager	**Scott Miller**
Cisco Marketing Program Manager	**Edie Quiroz**
Production Manager	**Patrick Kanouse**
Senior Development Editor	**Christopher Cleveland**
Senior Project Editor	**Sheri Cain**
Copy Editor	**Marianne Madeiros**
Technical Editor(s)	**David Fellows, Doug Jones**
Team Coordinator	**Tammi Barnett**
Cover and Interior Designer	**Louisa Adair**
Composition	**Mark Shirar**
Indexer	**Tim Wright**

CISCO SYSTEMS

Corporate Headquarters	European Headquarters	Americas Headquarters	Asia Pacific Headquarters
Cisco Systems, Inc.	Cisco Systems International BV	Cisco Systems, Inc.	Cisco Systems, Inc.
170 West Tasman Drive	Haarlerbergpark	170 West Tasman Drive	Capital Tower
San Jose, CA 95134-1706	Haarlerbergweg 13-19	San Jose, CA 95134-1706	168 Robinson Road
USA	1101 CH Amsterdam	USA	#22-01 to #29-01
www.cisco.com	The Netherlands	www.cisco.com	Singapore 068912
Tel: 408 526-4000	www-europe.cisco.com	Tel: 408 526-7660	www.cisco.com
800 553-NETS (6387)	Tel: 31 0 20 357 1000	Fax: 408 527-0883	Tel: +65 6317 7777
Fax: 408 526-4100	Fax: 31 0 20 357 1100		Fax: +65 6317 7799

Cisco Systems has more than 200 offices in the following countries and regions. Addresses, phone numbers, and fax numbers are listed on the
Cisco.com Web site at www.cisco.com/go/offices.

Argentina • Australia • Austria • Belgium • Brazil • Bulgaria • Canada • Chile • China PRC • Colombia • Costa Rica • Croatia • Czech Republic
Denmark • Dubai, UAE • Finland • France • Germany • Greece • Hong Kong SAR • Hungary • India • Indonesia • Ireland • Israel • Italy
Japan • Korea • Luxembourg • Malaysia • Mexico • The Netherlands • New Zealand • Norway • Peru • Philippines • Poland • Portugal
Puerto Rico • Romania • Russia • Saudi Arabia • Scotland • Singapore • Slovakia • Slovenia • South Africa • Spain • Sweden
Switzerland • Taiwan • Thailand • Turkey • Ukraine • United Kingdom • United States • Venezuela • Vietnam • Zimbabwe

About the Author

DR. ROUZBEH YASSINI is the founder and CEO of YAS Broadband Ventures LLC of Andover, Massachusetts, a venture capital firm that provides capital financing, consulting services, and academic insight into the broadband industry. In 1990, he founded LANcity, which introduced the first high-speed residential communications modem that was designed to integrate with cable television networks. LANcity's successful introduction spawned a new consumer electronics technology category known as the cable modem, which today, is used in millions of households worldwide. He has gained an international reputation as a broadband visionary and has established cable modem technical standards through his support of industry initiatives at Cable Television Laboratories, Inc. In 1998, *CED Magazine* named Rouzbeh Yassini its Man of the Year, recognizing his contributions to the industry. He has been quoted in numerous business and trade periodicals and newspapers and is a frequent speaker at international conferences devoted to digital services and the broadband infrastructure.

About the Contributing Authors

STEWART SCHLEY is a writer and publishing executive with more than 21 years of experience. He has written and edited numerous business magazines and telecommunications industry reference books.

ROGER BROWN is the editorial director of Reed Business Information's Telecom Group, and a 17-year-veteran journalist in business and technology.

LESLIE ELLIS is a writer and author who has covered cable television technology and industry economics since 1987.

About the Technical Reviewers

DAVID FELLOWS is the chief technology officer at Comcast Cable Communications, responsible for technology, engineering, and centralized operations. He has held similar positions at ATT Broadband, MediaOne, RoadRunner, and Continental Cablevision. David is the chair of CableLabs' Technical Advisory Committee, which provides oversight to CableLabs' technical activities. He was the long-time chair of the DOCSIS Certification Board, which oversaw the development of cable modem specifications. He is chair of the SCTE's Data Standards Subcommittee, the ANSI-approved standards-setting body for cable modem, Voice over Internet Protocol, and home gateway standards for cable systems. He has served on numerous private and public company boards, as well as technical advisory boards, and has received a number of industry accolades, including the NCTA Vanguard Award, *CED Magazine's* Man of the Year, and *Telephony Magazine's* Fiber Optic Visionary.

DOUG JONES is chief architect at YAS Broadband Ventures, LLC. He oversees technology development for new telecommunications services, including IP telephony, high-speed data, digital video, and multimedia services over HFC networks, as well as emerging technologies in home networking. Prior to joining YAS, Doug served in engineering positions in both the cable and telephony industries working on video and data applications and services. He earned M.S.E.E and B.S.E.E. degrees from the University of Texas at Austin. He is a published author of a variety of magazine columns and technical papers presented at industry forums.

Dedications

Dedicated to Leslie, Roger, and Stewart. For writing it all down.

Acknowledgments

This book reflects my sincere belief that broadband technology can make planet Earth a better place to live. My hope is that helping more people understand the power of broadband will inspire greater real-life services, invention, and advances that make use of this powerful global communications technology.

In the creation of this book, I am especially indebted to my colleagues, friends, and reviewers David Fellows, Doug Jones, Susan Marshall, Seth Morrison, Paul Nikolich, Jay Rolls, Mike Schwartz, and Doug Semon. Also, to Sudhir Ispahani and Bob Cruickshank for their continuous support, and to Paul Bosco for his contributions in getting this book published.

I am further indebted to my many friends and associates in the industry who hail from a grand alphabet soup of organizations including myriad cable providers, CTAM, IEEE, IETF, ITU/UIT, NCTA, SCTE, and CableLabs, whose tireless efforts to forge an end-to-end specification for high-speed broadband service surely will benefit generations to come. Also, to the team at LANcity and YAS for their undivided loyalty, innovations, and pioneering foundations of broadband, and to the fine institution that is West Virginia University.

Finally, I will always be indebted to my family: Dad, Mom, Uncle Dr. Yassini, sister Pari, brother Sia, and, especially, Pam—friend, sister, believer, and the person without whom I would never have been able to do LANcity, YAS, or this book. She is there for me unconditionally, "24/7," to help with my dream. Thank you, Pam, and to all of my family, for the unconditional love, encouragement, inspiration, belief, and trust they have provided me for years as I have pursued the broadband dream.

—Rouzbeh

Table of Contents

Foreword

Planet Broadband covers the nascent history and status of the broadband movement. In doing so, it wrestles with the definition of broadband, discusses the various forms it's taking around the world, and suggests the possible futures it might have. I have known and worked with Rouzbeh Yassini and his contributors for over a decade, and, in a sense, we (and many others) have tried to discover what broadband is together. This book is a collection of their learnings, observations, and guesses.

Just over a decade ago, I saw an alpha-version of Mosaic—the first web browser. It struck me that the average cable customer could handle "point and click." But my focus was on the television set. I contacted Delphi in Cambridge, Massachusetts, and met with them to determine the feasibility of adding Internet and web access to an interactive TV service we had in trial at Continental Cablevision (GTE Mainstreet). The Delphi engineers persuaded me to focus instead on the personal computer. Basically, they all wanted high-speed Internet access themselves from their homes. Enter Rouzbeh and LANcity. Continental Cablevision was using some of his equipment to carry lottery data for the state of New Hampshire (LAN-to-LAN connectivity at native speed was the buzzword). Rouzbeh responded by forward pricing the modems for a launch, and the rest, as they say, is history.

But even a decade later, history is not clear on the subject. I am often asked whether broadband is all hype. My reply is if you expect it to change your life tomorrow morning, you may safely consider it all hype. You will do what you did over dialup, only faster and with more satisfaction. But in the longer term, it is not possible to over-hype it. Broadband will change everything about the way you are entertained, informed, educated, how you communicate, and schedule your life. Maybe even how you are governed. Broadband is the electricity of the information age. Before electricity, to light up your home, you lit fires and used candles (dialup). You also went to bed early! Civilized areas and expensive homes had gas lanterns (ISDN?). But electricity changed your way of life. It not only brought you light (the first "killer app"), but powered hundreds of devices—from washers and dryers to toasters to eventually fueling telecommunications.

It is an exciting time to be in telecommunications, but quite often, I wish we were a little smarter. I can tell that in the future, looking back on all this, it will be obvious what is going on. I assure you that in the thick of things, we have little clue what we are hatching. Maybe my colleagues at the telephone companies know more (and aren't saying) about the broadband world, but I doubt it. If we look to another shift from narrowband to broadband, radio to television, TV has progressed from theater over the air, to soap operas and sitcoms. And now to reality shows. Broadband started with e-mail and web pages, and has progressed in under a decade to peer-to-peer applications and to multi-player games with audio and video chat to teammates. The latter feels like a reality show, starring you as one of the participants, especially if you like shoot-'em-up games.

This broaches the question of what content is in the broadband age. With cable TV, content comes from studios (largely in Hollywood) and is purchased wholesale and sold retail by cable companies. Content is generated in one place, and consumed by many users—typically at the same time (tune in at 8 P.M. tonight for *Friends*!). With telephone companies, the content is the phone call, and is generated, in a sense, by the participants themselves. It is one-to-one, and the content is generated at the edge of the network. Broadband spans a spectrum of content meanings. You have online service providers, including the portal of your Internet service provider. It is authored centrally and comes with advertising, same as television programs. So it smells like traditional content. But you also have e-mail, analogous to the phone call, where the participants generate the content. Web logs and personal web pages all are content generated at the edge of the network, but generated once and viewed by many (the hope is!). Online games are in between—there is a central authoring and often a hosting function, but the participants play a key role, also. You can see advertising take on multiple roles. When a pop-up ad interrupts your web search for the weather ("Buy a book on weather at Amazon.com!"), it resembles traditional advertising. But when you go to Ford's website to look up information on a model you are thinking of buying, then look at the inventory of a local dealership, there is a lot of selling going on, but it does not feel the same as advertising. With broadcast, multicast, and unicast models, broadband spans traditional models for content and communication.

Along with the uncertainties in the content and services enabled by broadband is the definition of broadband itself. I believe that broadband is a set of capabilities, not the speed of a single pipe. Video-on-demand at Comcast includes movies-on-demand (pay $3.99 and get to watch a movie with pause and rewind), subscription-on-demand (subscribe to Showtime, and for no extra fee, or a small fixed fee, see a set of content provided by Showtime), and free-on-demand (included in the price of a digital tier is a set of programming-on-demand for no extra fee). We have personal video recorders built into set-tops that allow a customer to store videos for later viewing, and we also have some live programming stored in the network as part of the free-on-demand service. By the end of this year, both PVR and VoD will have high-definition TV content available. But these capabilities are hard to summarize in a single speed number—the usual way that narrowband is differentiated from broadband.

The definition of broadband may be an academic exercise; the marketplace will determine what it will pay for various data rates, symmetries, and capabilities (services enabled). But it may not. There is an effort to convince the government that ubiquitous broadband availability should be a national priority. It seems a little early to be discussing the government stepping in for a number of reasons: First, cable systems, egged on by Telco DSL competition and by countering DBS video competition (in an effort to offer services they can't), are doing a pretty good job of covering the country. In the case of Comcast, we will have a third of the country covered by the end of 2004. Secondly, the actual benefit to the customer is not defined. What services are possible with a symmetric service, or unshared service, that are not possible over today's DSL or cable-modem service? And at what price?

What is broadband anyway? Read on to find out.

David Fellows
CTO
Comcast Cable Communications

Introduction

Planet Broadband examines the promise and prowess behind the fastest-growing communications technology since the cellular telephone. It's broadband: high-speed access to a world of interactive digital media and communications. *Planet Broadband* explains why broadband is more than just a better connection to the Internet—and how broadband promises to touch and improve on nearly every aspect of modern-day life.

As the inventor of the first commercial cable modem, author Rouzbeh Yassini has seen first-hand how broadband can propel positive changes in society. From access to education to improvements in our environment and working lives, broadband is a new alphabet that will unlock the real power of the information age. *Planet Broadband* educates and inspires people to make use of this powerful new tool in positive ways.

Who Should Read This Book?

Planet Broadband is written for curious, active participants in the new information-age economy. From filmmakers to philanthropists, entrepreneurs to educators, broadband poses enormous new opportunities for prosperity and progress. *Planet Broadband* offers these individuals a roadmap to the future—an easy-to-digest manual that helps people understand a new technological force that is literally reshaping the way we work, learn, live, and play.

How This Book Is Organized

Chapter 1, "Broadband: Anything, Anywhere, Anytime"—An informative and provocative description of broadband—the missing link that finally delivers the promise of the information age to millions of global citizens.

Chapter 2, "Broadband's Birth"—The onset of a new medium explained in easy-to-understand language, going behind the scenes and beyond the hype to show you how and why broadband began.

Chapter 3, "The Broadband Bazaar"—An examination of the two most common broadband delivery platforms—telephone-line DSL connections and high-speed cable modems—plus differences and strengths of each.

Chapter 4, "Who Gets Broadband?"—A review of broadband penetration trends in leading-edge countries across Europe and the Asia-Pacific region, and why coalitions of government and industry around the world are pressing hard to realize aggressive deployment rates for broadband.

Chapter 5, "The Broadband Home"—Compelling research and fascinating anthropology that provides a clear picture of exactly how broadband is already changing the lives of millions of users every day.

Chapter 6, "Planet Broadband"—Why the environmental promises of the information age have fallen short—and why broadband is the glue that finally will bring them about, transforming definitions of work and improving productivity at the same time.

Chapter 7, "Broadband Content"—A concise exploration of the efforts being made today in the content industries to harness the power of broadband for the benefit of producers and consumers alike, with interviews from emerging content kings such as RealNetworks and Walt Disney Internet Group.

Chapter 8, "Broadband Everywhere"—An irrefutable argument for broadband as the centerpiece of our next great economic wave and a key to economic vitality and social health.

CHAPTER 1

BROADBAND:
ANYTHING, ANYWHERE, ANYTIME

THERE IS SOMETHING BIG happening out there. It's about connectivity and data and communicating, and it is changing the lives of average citizens just as surely as the automobile, the telephone, and electricity changed the lives of preceding generations.

Today, it's possible for a surgeon to check on a patient's cholesterol and enzyme levels not by taking a blood sample in the office, but by reading a data file transmitted from the home. Video gaming enthusiasts can battle in real-time against opponents who live hundreds, even thousands, of miles away. A busy professional, alerted to the arrival of a utility bill by an audible chime from her kitchen computer, can review the invoice, pay it, and record the transaction within the time it takes to heat water for afternoon tea. The video clip of a young ballplayer's home run from this afternoon's baseball game is available this evening for enjoyment by the child's grandparents who live halfway across the globe. An electronic field trip takes students through museums and concert halls once accessible only through an in-person visit.

The force behind this transformation of daily life and social interaction is something called *broadband*: high-speed, always-on connectivity to an interactive digital network. Five years ago, the term was barely circulated beyond the test laboratories and war rooms of telecommunications and data-networking engineers. Now, it is no longer a term reserved solely for those in the technology trenches. Broadband has entered the daily lexicon, and most people have at least a cursory idea of what it's about. Even a magazine on the newsstands showcases the way people are using broadband to change the way they work, play, and live. More to the point, broadband is rapidly infiltrating the world's community of Internet users. In the U.S., more than a third of all Internet users now surf the web using a broadband connection, says the research firm Nielsen//NetRatings. In Hong Kong, a stunning 82 percent of home Internet users are operating at broadband speed. Forty percent of France's Internet population is now hooked on broadband. The numbers continue to rise: From 2001 to 2002, the number of U.S. Internet users with broadband increased by 60 percent, while the number of people with old-fashioned dialup connections to the Internet fell by 10 percent.

In a way, this creature called broadband is the embodiment of a rusty old concept once called the information highway; or, depending on the level of fervor exhibited or caffeine ingested by the evangelist, the information superhighway. Understandably, the populace has soured on this phrase. Said highway was promised by a whole phalanx of industry and government officials beginning in the early 1990s, and its failure to appear on schedule has tarnished the concept. By now, the world was supposed to be basking in the joys of electronic newspapers, TV sets that might summon up any program anytime, and telephones that displayed video images just as crisply as they reproduced human voices. A quick survey of the landscape suggests those sorts of applications remain the stuff of far-fetched techno-dreaming, at least in the average household. The information highway appears not to have been made accessible to the masses just yet.

Or perhaps it has arrived and we're just not looking in the right places. Those with a perceptive eye know change is afoot. More quietly and in a more scattered fashion than the headlines once trumpeted, interesting ideas, such as video-on-demand and video telephones, are in fact sprouting up. Content once reserved for a tiny elite is now available at the click of a button to millions of average citizens in the U.S. and beyond. The nightly news delivered to audiences in far-away countries can be summoned within the homes of emigrants who live halfway across the world. Homeowners are buying up tiny video cameras that allow them to keep watch over the household while vacationing at the beach. Broadband connectivity has taken the personal computer out of the study and planted it in the kitchen and the family room, where it invites more frequent bursts of usage throughout the day—a pattern researchers call "information snacking." Different behaviors and communications patterns are emerging within the busy lives of people across the globe.

Ten years after U.S. Vice President Albert Gore appeared before the Washington Press Club to talk about something he called the information highway, the key access ramps are not only constructed, but are attracting more and more traffic every day. Unlike the great physical interstate highways of the 1950s, they have been built with private investment—hundreds of billions of dollars of capital expended to transform cable television and telephone networks into high-speed data conduits. Building out a data infrastructure that will support dazzling new communications possibilities has taken longer than some might have been led to believe when Gore made his seminal 1993 speech. Broadband's engineers have encountered twists and turns both of fate and economics. Participants and would-be participants in the broadband transformation have both succeeded and failed spectacularly. There have been no single celebratory events or ribbon-cutting ceremonies to mark its debut. Like the Internet itself, the high-speed information highway has arisen in an unpredictable, collaboratively conceived way. Yet absent some of the early fanfare and hype that once accompanied it, the information highway is in fact up and running. Today, it goes by the popular name of broadband.

Credit for broadband's ascension goes to several places. The U.S. Defense Department's Advanced Research Project Agency (ARPA), of course, developed fundamental data networking techniques and architectures that inspired today's Internet. The personal computer industry's persistence in making ever more powerful machines available at steadily decreasing prices has democratized access to powerful information tools. Content creators, inspired by the possibilities of a new medium, have propelled demand for better, faster Internet connectivity by developing increasingly elaborate and rich expressions of ideas and entertainment available in digital form. Telecommunications regulatory policy in the U.S. and elsewhere has sparked a wave of activity and investment. Most importantly, cable television, telephone, and wireless network companies have reengineered their networks to support extremely fast data rates. Today, about 45 million residences across the world are outfitted with broadband access ramps enabling the Internet to become something ARPA inventors could scarcely have dreamed about in the late 1960s: a medium through which virtually any manner of digital content can flow.

The Internet @ Broadband Speed

If broadband is making its way to the forefront of everyday life, the initial credit belongs to a sprawling *uber*-network of computers, file servers, and protocols. This network is the gracious host that has introduced broadband to everyday citizens. It is called, of course, the Internet. To date, what's thought of as broadband generally has been wrapped up in the cloak of high-speed Internet access. Broadband has become known to the general populace as a means of accessing the Internet at faster data rates than traditional dialup modems and slow-moving delivery networks permit.

But in truth, broadband is more than that. Broadband is the lever that will twist and bend our existing concepts of media and communications into something that is new and different.

Thanks to broadband, our current array of information appliances—the television set, the computer, the radio, the digital camcorder—will begin to display new possibilities that previously were unthinkable. The personal library of jazz CDs that you have carefully arranged in the corner of the family room will become a relic. Not because your musical tastes will change dramatically, but because your music—the library of selections you enjoy and collect—will be freed from its current imprisonment on physical discs and tapes. Broadband connectivity will mean that your own personal library is accessible to you from an invisible constellation of files that you can summon at will—whether you're traveling in New York City or enjoying the sunset on your patio.

Broadband will find a myriad of ways to enter your life. When your phone rings, you'll know who's calling because your television set will display their name. When you want to watch the nightly news, you will decide when it starts, and you'll pause it in mid-stream whenever you want. Instead of reading e-mail messages, you'll hear them: It will be just as easy for your friend to send you a recorded voice message as a text message. The framed photograph of your nephews and nieces that hangs on the wall will change as soon as they upload a new image taken earlier that day from their vacation at the beach. The location where you do your office work might not be your office, but your home. Even if you do continue to commute to work, broadband will make it easier to do so. Upon learning that traffic is backed up for miles on the freeway, your broadband command center will alert your alarm clock to ring 20 minutes earlier than usual and will instruct your coffeemaker to begin brewing on the same schedule. (But don't ask broadband to do it all. You'll have to remember to place the coffee in the filter on your own the night before.)

Over time, broadband will come to be known as more than just a way to get the Internet to work faster on your computer. Broadband will become the underlying platform for almost every conceivable media, entertainment, and communications application that touches the lives of average citizens on a daily basis. Broadband will course through everyday life with the same permanence and ubiquity now associated with electricity and running water. It will come to be associated with a wide array of devices, from the television set in the family room to the telephone in the study, to some type of device in the car that hasn't even been invented yet. If some dreamers have their way, it will even find its way into the kitchen refrigerator.

These are all intoxicating ideas, and they typify the excitement and innovation that's percolating in the broadband communications industries. Still, many times before, proponents have been guilty of saddling new technologies with a similar sort of enthusiastic spin, placing upon them the weight of an impossible burden whose failure to materialize leaves us wanting. In fact, some of the promises associated with broadband bear a familiar and unrequited ring. In 1912, the futurist S.C. Gilfillan, commenting on the adoption of the telephone, predicted that, by 1940, our homes would be fully outfitted with living-room theaters allowing us to dial up three-dimensional Shakespearean plays and summon entire symphonies at will. Of course, it took decades for phone companies merely to provide reliable dial-tone service and eliminate line failures. Meanwhile, the living-room Shakespeare is still waiting. It is true that, in today's enthusiasm over broadband, one can hear echoes from the premature fantasies of technologies past.

Yet the truth is that communications technologies that change the character of daily life tend to come at us not in one fell swoop, but from the periphery, gaining momentum and eventually achieving a sort of critical penetration. It is doubtful that any reader of this page doesn't own a color television set, a videocassette recorder, and a personal computer. Each device has made its mark on the way we work, relax, learn things, and communicate. Yet none of these technologies made its way into ubiquity overnight. Broadband is following a similar progression as these other requisites of modern life, which makes it reasonable to project that broadband will achieve the same sort of presence in our lives. Table 1-1 illustrates the technology adoption rate based on historical fact.

Table 1-1 *Adoption Time for New Technologies, U.S.*

	Years to Reach 10 Percent Adoption	**Years to Reach 50 Percent Adoption**
Videocassette recorder	10	14
Compact disc player	4.5	10.5
Color TV	12	18
Cellular phone	8	15
Personal computer	4	18
Broadband	4	—

Source: Federal Communications Commission, April 2002.

Rising Power

So why the fanfare now? Because even in the present, broadband is already making a statement. Taken as an instrument purely of Internet access, broadband is rising in power and influence, and its growth signals legitimate enthusiasm over its possibilities within the global population. After all, broadband isn't free. People generally pay the equivalent of $40 to $50 each month for the privilege of a broadband connection, and the number of people electing to make that investment is growing at a breakneck rate. One research group, In-Stat/MDR, estimates that worldwide residential broadband subscribers had climbed to 46 million by the end of 2002. The numbers impress because of how rapidly they have sprouted, considering that broadband only became commercially available on a large scale in 1999. In the year 2001 alone, the number of broadband subscribers in developed countries doubled to slightly more than 31 million, according to a report by the Organization for Economic

Cooperation and Development (OECD). By the end of 2002, the organization affirmed other estimates that the world had more than 40 million broadband customers. Guessing what the future holds for broadband adoption is just that—guesswork—but no signs show a momentum slowdown yet. In-Stat/MDR, projects worldwide residential broadband subscribers to soar to more than 60 million by the end of 2003, and to double again by 2006 to more than 130 million. As the chief operating officer of Sony Corp., Kunitake Ando, stated during an industry speech, "…the broadband wave will wash over us, and it is coming fast."

How these growing numbers of users receive their broadband service is a testament to the changing face of communications networks. Broadband requires a new type of communications infrastructure, and in its early gestation, it is making use of existing networks, particularly cable television and telephone networks, in new ways. Of the 40 million-plus residential broadband customers estimated by the end of 2002, a slight majority (21.9 million) were served by digital subscriber line (DSL), which is a type of broadband offering associated with the telephone network; another 18.6 million were fed by cable television networks; and the remaining 2.2 million were served by wireless and other distribution networks.

As Table 1-2 shows, the broadband explosion is everywhere. At the end of 2002, the U.S. had more total broadband users than any other country—close to 17 million—but the broadband experience had infiltrated several countries much deeper than it had in the U.S.

Table 1-2 *Broadband Subscribers by Country*

Country	DSL Subscribers	Cable Modem Subscribers	Other	Total	Broadband Subscribers per 100 Inhabitants
Australia	111,800	140,900	8,500	261,200	1.4
Austria	136,000	207,800		343,800	4.2
Belgium	362,000	259,036	23,824	644,860	6.3
Canada	1,330,800	1,848,000		3,178,800	10.3
Czech Republic	100	12,000		12,100	0.12
Denmark	233,000	121,789	784	355,573	6.7
Finland	71,738	41,000		112,738	2.2
France	730,000	233,579		963,579	1.6
Germany	2,500,000	39,100	50,000	2,589,100	3.2

Table 1-2   *Broadband Subscribers by Country (Continued)*

Country	DSL Subscribers	Cable Modem Subscribers	Other	Total	Broadband Subscribers per 100 Inhabitants
Greece	72	0		72	0.0
Hungary	18,781	19,200		37,981	0.4
Iceland	12,900	0	500	13,400	4.8
Ireland	1,200	800		2,000	0.05
Italy	585,000	0		585,000	1.2
Japan	3,300,926	1,626,000	87,100	5,014,026	4.0
Korea	5,734,690	3,287,464	36,363	9,058,517	19.2
Luxembourg	2,670	15		2,685	0.6
Mexico	51,786	15,000		66,786	0.07
Netherlands	192,000	432,400	200	624,600	3.9
New Zealand	39,000	4,500		43,500	1.1
Norway	75,000	46,300	6379	127,679	2.8
Poland	4,000	10,700		14,700	0.038
Portugal	5,203	143,333		148,536	1.5
Slovak Republic	0	420		420	0.01
Spain	660,861	180,191		841,052	2.1
Sweden	344,000	127,600	128,000	599,600	6.8
Switzerland	101,777	180,000		281,777	3.9
Turkey	2,971	11,920		14,711	0.022
United Kingdom	299,000	452,994	2,000	753,994	1.3
United States	5,082,865	9,200,000	1,785,406	16,068,271	5.8
Totals	**21,990,140**	**18,642,041**	**2,129,056**	**42,761,237**	

Source: Analysis of data published by OECD (Organization for Economic Cooperation and Development), 2002.

Since this comprehensive survey, broadband has continued to produce impressive growth. In the U.S., more than 50,000 new households connect to broadband *every week*. Based on current trends, it's possible that broadband will find its way into a majority of American homes within the next five years. By comparison, it took 70 years for the telephone to make its way into 60 percent of homes, and it was only after 90 years that a majority of U.S. residents had their own automobile. The pace of change has quickened.

The growing consumer embrace of broadband is important because it establishes a foundation for the future. As the broadband footprint expands, it creates an underlying user base and economic footing that will spur the next generations of service. What passes as a superior means for Internet access today will migrate to a much broader electronic firmament in the future.

The seeds of this broader realm of possibility are already being planted. As discussed more elaborately later, broadband is recreating the Internet, transforming it from a medium of text and photographs to a medium of video and sound, and a rich multimedia intermingling. And that's only for starters. Broadband is an enabler. It makes the Internet come alive in new and exciting ways.

But to examine broadband in detail requires first a basic definition. At its core, broadband is a means for communicating in the language of digital media, over very fast networks, with something we call *always-on* connectivity.

The Need for Speed

How fast? For now, it is safe to say a digital network that renders data at a rate of at least one megabit per second (or 1 Mbps in the parlance of digital networking), ought to make the broadband cut. One Mbps means one million bits of digital information are hurtled through the broadband pipe every second. A *bit* represents an elemental expression of information in the digital world, representing one of two values, 1 or 0. Molded into patterns identifiable to computers, combinations of bits can come to represent things. The character *h* within this document, for example, is recognized by a computer as a combination of several bits. The color and brightness of a tiny fraction of a photographic image depicted over a computer screen also can be composed of a series of bits, and so, too, can be the gentle warble of a falsetto voice transmitted over a digital network.

So 1 Mbps it is, at least for now. For comparison's sake, 1 Mbps is enough speed to make basic Internet browsing a much more palatable experience than it is in the world of slow-moving, narrowband connections. At 1 Mbps, data travel to your computer nearly 20 times faster than if you had a typical dialup modem that tops out at 56 kilobits per second (kbps)—the most common speed for most residential Internet users today. Dense graphics and modest audio and video applications work acceptably at 1 Mbps. A file that used to take minutes to download now takes only a few seconds. The frustration of sluggish page displays is replaced by a responsive, satisfying performance. True, over time, you'll want a much faster supply of digital information. It's possible that in your lifetime, you will enjoy digital media and communications services that, fed through a fiber-optic network, zip their way to your home at 100 Mbps or faster. That's enough speed to handle anything the world can throw your way, from high-definition video to you-are-there virtual replicas of the world's great art museums. Already, terrestrial broadcast, satellite, and cable television providers are delivering high-definition television signals to new-age TV sets at per-channel data rates of 10 Mbps or more. But for now, the leap from a 56-kbps modem to a 1-Mbps broadband connection is enough to provoke glorious cries of "Hallelujah!" from those who have suffered through the tedium of what some have labeled the "World Wide Wait."

Those unfamiliar with data rates or kilobits or those who assume megabits are a brand name for super-potent vitamins need not fear. These slices of digital vocabulary are purely expressions of speed, which characterizes the rate information flows over a digital network, no different in semantic intent than the highway signs that display the permissible speed limit as motorists zoom along to their destinations. But to understand broadband requires a basic familiarity with one of its hallmarks, which is the speed of data throughput.

Why be so persnickety about things? Because it is important to rally around a general agreement of what constitutes a broadband experience, and absent a trustworthy and measurable standard of reference, the lines can get awfully murky. Until now, there has been little agreement about where the dividing line between broadband and *narrowband* (slow and tedious) service can be found. Curiously, for as much as the word *broadband* is used lately, finding an agreed-upon definition is like trying to capture a stream of water by hand.

The U.S. Federal Communications Commission says anything less than 200 kilobits (200,000 bits per second) should not be considered an example of an advanced digital network. Others, rightly so, demand more, looking forward to the day when the average home enjoys head-spinning data delivery speeds now reserved for giant corporations and powerful government agencies.

Some nations already are ahead of the game. The world's broadband leader, at least measured by the percentage of residents who use broadband, is South Korea. There, close to 10 million households—70 percent of the nation's residences—are connected to broadband networks delivering data rates of 8 Mbps. Broadband development is still in the early stages in most advanced nations, however, and the idea of a 1 Mbps standard has yet to take hold with a majority of Internet users.

In the U.S., newspaper ads for residential DSL networks, one of the popular flavors of broadband, occasionally tout data rates in the 200- to 600-kbps range as broadband. The cable TV industry, currently the largest U.S. provider of broadband services, is introducing new pricing and delivery schemes that allow users to choose the data rate they prefer, with entry-level options as low as 200 kbps. No doubt all of these offerings will be christened broadband, despite their relatively less impressive performance.

Worse still, some people misguidedly use "broadband" to describe any type of digital information that moves over a network. Irritating and poorly rendered video clips that appear on a computer screen, the size of a postage stamp, are somehow labeled examples of broadband. During a recent visit to the heart of what is still, despite the dot.com crash, a hotbed of information technology innovation— California's Silicon Valley—a clerk at a hotel proudly proclaimed the availability of "broadband" in a room. In fact, the only connection available was a telephone line available to plug into a slow-moving dialup modem.

The absence of any shared, consistent definition of a broadband data standard attests to the fact that broadband is apt to take on many shapes and forms over time. In fact, for some applications, such as sending e-mail or instant-messages, little meaningful improvement is rendered at data rates higher than what most dialup users currently experience. Digital television signals, in contrast, are relative bandwidth hogs, requiring a steady supply of 3 Mbps or more. Over time, broadband applications will share a common need for a certain minimal data benchmark, but will vary widely in their actual consumption of bandwidth. Or perhaps broadband will always be a relative term meaning faster data rates than those common in the recent past.

Data Rates in the Real World

Most experienced car drivers have developed an internal understanding of the relationship between a mathematical measure of speed and the physical correlation. We understand that at 15 miles per hour, we're meandering calmly among suburban streets. At 75 mph, we're cruising fast.

We're nowhere near that level of intuition when it comes to data rates—the engineer's expression of how fast digital messages travel.

The parlance can be mind-numbing to the newcomer. Is 4 Mbps faster than 128 kbps? (Yes, by a long shot.) Is my business/office T-1 network emblematic of what my home broadband experience will be? (Probably not; most cable-modem services surpass what a T-1 delivers, speed-wise.)

One of the easy litmus tests is whether the information appearing on a computer renders itself faster than a user can read or type. If the user has to stop and wait for the information to catch up, that's not broadband. If it looks, sounds or feels like the Internet experience of old; that is, a slow-moving, tedious and unreliable connection to web pages, e-mail and streaming media, it is not broadband. If it is a struggle to decipher the words a friend is saying through a new kind of phone connection, it's not broadband.

The frustrated web surfer, accustomed to waiting for pages to render and data downloads to complete their journey, is often thrilled to encounter a true broadband experience for the first time. A lightbulb, in effect, goes on, and the user is apt to repeat a line similar to that announced by actress Geena Davis in the 1991 Metro-Goldwyn Mayer movie *Thelma & Louise*: "Now I understand what all the fuss is about." She wasn't talking about broadband, but the point is made.

That said, know that one million bits per second is an impressive opening feat. Over time, broadband networks available to the average homeowner or apartment dweller, or even hotel patron, will leave the 1 Mbps reference standard in the digital dust, of course, just as relentless advances in computer processing have turned the once-mighty Intel 486 processor into a relic of silicon past. The time will come when a student of broadband history dusts off the cover of this book and chuckles in amusement at the quaint notion that the world once survived on data rates as feeble as 1 Mbps. But it is a starting point, and to judge against it, remember that in the early 1990s, it seemed perfectly reasonable to become excited about an upgrade in data transmission speed to the then-astonishing rate of 28.8 kilobytes per second, or 28 K in shorthand.

Table 1-3 shows how much raw speed one organization, Canada's National Broadband Task Force, believes we need for various tasks we might perform over a broadband network to the home.

Table 1-3   *Suggested Data Rates for Broadband Network Tasks*

Task	Suggested Data Rate (Bits Per Second)
Teleworking	7 Mbps (7,000,000 bits per second)
Videoconferencing	800 kbps (800,000 bits per second)
E-learning	7 Mbps
Telemedicine	7 Mbps
Videophone	200 kbps
Movies-on-demand	7 Mbps
Audio-on-demand	700 kbps
Telegames	600 kbps
Electronic banking	400 kbps
Digital television	7 Mbps

Source: National Broadband Task Force, Canada, 2002.

The task force is suggesting that certain applications, such as audio-on-demand or home banking, can perform ably at speeds of less than 1 Mbps. The fact is, expressions of data rate alone don't tell the entire story; differences and capabilities related to the processing power of computers and other network devices play a big role in determining the broadband experience. Even so, the real power of broadband is more than summoning up today's radio news report whenever the mood strikes, or transferring funds to a checking account at 2 a.m. Ultimately, broadband will provide for a vast range of media, entertainment, and communications applications. Many of these applications simply don't perform at certain speeds.

The national broadband connectivity goal some proponents are beginning to suggest is at least 10 Mbps to the home—or 200 times faster than today's typical dialup Internet connections and more than 10 times faster than many of today's early broadband residential and business networks. Enough capacity so that, coupled with the right sorts of devices and intelligent network management schemes, it can supply whatever a user wants: great-looking video to the TV set, crystal-clear voices over a telephone, entire libraries waiting to be summoned on a portable display in your bedroom or study. The convergence of technology, economics, and public policy isn't yet at hand to support delivery of 10 Mbps interactive networks to the average home. Estimates of the amount of new investment required to bring about a substantially more robust and capable broadband infrastructure in the U.S. alone start at $100 billion and rise from there. But even today as broadband begins to take root in the general populace, it is recognized that substantial improvements in data rates and availability are essential to deliver on the broadband promise. "A review of existing and likely technologies…suggests that we have only achieved the first level of broadband speeds," said a May 2002 report published by U.S. Senator Joseph Lieberman, who introduced a wide-ranging bill designed to promote broadband service infrastructure. "On the foreseeable horizon are technologies that offer advanced broadband speeds of 10 Mbps in the near-term, and 100 Mbps in the medium-term. Arguably, it will be at these advanced speed ranges that the greatest benefits from broadband will come," the report states.

The Always-On Network

Speed matters, but there is another core definition of what makes a data connection a broadband connection. In addition to its definition purely by speed, broadband also can be defined by its ubiquitous presence. It's always on. This means that, when a user fires up whatever it is he wants to do, whether it's browsing the current online weather report or zinging a video clip to a colleague in Singapore, the network that accomplishes the task is at the ready. No dialing up, no waiting to "boot," no fidgeting with settings. Broadband literally means the network is up, running, and ready all the time. The term *always-on* refers to this sort of ready availability, and it is used often in descriptions of broadband. Correspondingly, as broadband becomes increasingly deployed, we will less frequently use the term online. With broadband, as with electricity and running water, rarely is there a moment when the supply isn't available. In a manner of speaking, broadband users are always online.

Those who study the behaviors of broadband users tend to walk away pointing to the always-on aspect of broadband as a more profound influence than the speed of the connection. If you already have a broadband connection in your own home, you've almost certainly changed the way you interact with the Internet because of the always-on nature of your access.

In five or ten years, it will seem naïve that a book written in 2003 pointed to an "always-on" communications spigot, as opposed to the hiss and scratch of a dialup Internet connection, as an indication of great progress. In most developed nations, children born after 1994 will never have known a time when there wasn't a World Wide Web. Similarly, with broadband gaining market presence at rapid speed, children born from this point forward will come to view "always-on" broadband connectivity as something as common as cold water from the tap.

With always-on access, the relationship between people and the Internet changes in interesting ways from the behavior typified by dialup users. As this book discusses later, people with broadband connections tend to snack away at what the Internet has to offer by accessing the network more frequently, sometimes for short bursts of activity, other times for elongated and fruitful sessions. The Pew Internet & American Life Project, which attempts to chronicle the influence of the Internet on everyday citizens, reported in a comprehensive 2002 study that people with broadband connections not only spend more total time using the Internet, but do different things over it:

> "When asked what they have done *most* online since getting a home broadband connection, a plurality (32 percent) responded, 'looking for information' with e-mailing a close second (28 percent)," the report said. "Users also say they have spent more time online since getting broadband (61 percent say they do)."

A barely born newcomer on the communications scene, broadband is already wreaking havoc with customary ways and established rules. Broadband is weaving itself into daily life and economic and social conventions. It has been invited into the homes of millions of global citizens and has quickly ingratiated itself into their lives, influencing the way they work, communicate, travel, gather information, stay in touch with families and friends, and more. Look no further than a teenage music fan with a revved-up DSL connection or a cable modem to exemplify the disruptive effect broadband has on traditional ways. Behind the techno-lingo of the new generation of music consumers—references to MP3s and ripping music to hard drives—there's a clear message that when it comes to consuming entertainment, the world is a new and unfamiliar place, wherein recorded music is enjoyed from altogether different sources than vinyl records and store-bought CDs. An invisible energy force of data packets, networks, protocols, and modulation schemes—the underlying technology of broadband—is changing the game. Understanding more about this emerging force is important not just to the people who distribute music for a living (although goodness knows they're struggling to get a grip on broadband), but to anybody who cares about the direction of media, communications, and social organization in the coming generations.

History in the Making

It is on that grand scale that the beginnings of broadband come into view. Rarely is it apparent in the immediate present that history—the dynamics and changes writers will later come to identify as key inflection points—is forming itself. In July of 1903, when the Ford Motor Company sold its first car (a two-cylinder Model A from its plant in Detroit, Michigan), not even the most observant could have conceived that vast highways and road systems would crisscross our lands, distributing passengers and cargo, and serving as the centerpiece of modern transportation. When Benjamin Franklin launched a kite into the sky during a thunderstorm 250 years ago, observers would have been hard-pressed to imagine entire communities laced with networks that bring electricity to light homes and literally power an entire economy. Today, it is common to take for granted the products of invention and discoveries so profound that they have reshaped civilization. These conveniences are so commonplace that by now they barely earn our attention on a daily basis.

So it will be with broadband. To the grandchildren of the present-day reader, new services that depend on broadband will have become so commonplace that nobody will give them much thought. Yet their onset will astound those who have grown up in the familiar world of today's communications networks. Twenty years from now, thanks to broadband, there won't be a separately identifiable "telephone network" as we know today. There won't be a separate "cable television" delivery system. There will be a network of broadband networks that manage, with equal grace and acumen, telephone calls and TV programs, and an entire range of services barely imaginable today.

Broadband will bring new categories of services to the world, turning traditional ways and models upside down. What were once disconnected services will become integrated. Here are some examples:

- On television, the idea of organizing programs and content into linear channels will fade, supplanted by the availability of a sea of personalized content, available anytime for the viewing.

- There will be little or no distinction between voice-mail and e-mail. There will simply be messages available for retrieval regardless of how a user connects.

- There will no longer be a distinction between a user's home telephone, mobile telephone, and e-mail account. Instead, users will be connected by a device that can reach them with voice, video, and text messages, all of them riding a broadband conduit to their destination.

- Display devices connected to broadband won't be singularly devoted to a particular task. A device might be used to watch a high-definition video movie one minute, and to check how much time is left for the pizza to cook the next.

The essential promise of broadband for future generations is to do away with current distinctions among networks. Technology thus far has produced a wealth of extremely capable, yet largely discreet access networks, such as the wireline telephone network and the wireless telephone network, or, in the video segment, several different networks for delivering video (cable, satellite and over-the-air broadcasting, to name the main three, followed inevitably by wireless networks). These distinctions will blur as broadband evolves to allow any properly outfitted network to connect the user to the same content and communications. Broadband will infiltrate not only the external networks—those that yank down entertainment content, the nightly news, and phone calls from relatives in distant places—but internal premises networks such as those that will instruct the alarm clock to snooze and tell the coffee maker to wait 15 minutes before brewing.

The beginnings of this homogenization are apparent even today, as distinctions among prevailing access networks are blurring. Cable television networks built originally to deliver TV channels now carry telephone calls and Internet content. The majority of the signal traffic across the telephone network now is devoted to digital data, not analog voice conversations. Even the networks that deliver electrical power to homes and businesses are going broadband as utility companies study ways to turn everyday electrical outlets into powerful broadband connection points.

The onset of the broadband age is now forming a future that is unimaginable to most. Humans in advanced nations have lived on this earth for the last 500 years as an industrial collective, lifted to new heights by the awesome might of machines and mechanics. Pistons, engines, levers, and factories harnessing the power of mass production have expanded our grasp, enabled us to manipulate and reform our physical environment, and supported new models for social organization.

Long chronicled and much studied, the industrial age represented the first wholesale transformation of civilization. Before this era, and literally since humanity began, we lived as an agricultural civilization, surviving for thousands of years by directing our physical energy toward the land itself.

The new age, today's age, has often been described as the age of information or the age of knowledge. The world has been instructed so many times that it is living in an age of information that the very words might cause a reader's eyes to blur and an internal alarm system to sound: Oh no, here we go again, a lecture about the information revolution. But something is different now. A new ingredient is being added to the mix in the form of broadband.

In the broadband age, the ways we communicate, collaborate, and conduct commerce—the three "Cs" of our society—will change. They will change because of broadband. Broadband is the new influence that is reshaping our daily lives. Broadband will create a new infrastructure that supports our economy and allows us to survive and flourish on the planet through the remainder of this century and beyond.

Fuel for the Info Age

Exactly what's new in this picture? Even casual readers recognize that the idea of an information age has been conceived and anticipated since the 1970s. The stunning arrival of the World Wide Web as a mass medium in the 1990s only furthered the fact that we are a civilization awash in a great sea of accessible information. What's new is that the fuel for this information age is only now beginning to become available. Just as refined oil has served to propel the cargo of our highways and transportation networks, broadband will propel our information networks.

William Kennard, a former chairman of the U.S. Federal Communications Commission, is among the many leaders who have watched broadband arrive on the scene, and been impressed by its potential. Says Kennard:

> "As we leave the Industrial Age and enter the Information Age, it's clear that despite all the technical advances and globalization, the formula for economic success has remained the same: economic prosperity relies on high-speed access to the critical network of information and commerce. That network is the Internet, and the type of access needed is broadband."

Elsewhere, the clarion call for broadband is just as audible. Canada's National Broadband Task Force proclaims that, "As a matter of urgency…all Canadians should have access to broadband network services so that they can live and prosper in any part of the land and have access to high levels of education, health, cultural and economic opportunities."

Proponents believe broadband will unleash the dispersal of knowledge and the ready ability to communicate knowledge. We might be entering an age in which information and knowledge prevail as the key drivers of societies and their economies, but it is the broadband revolution that will make it all come together.

Still, without dreamers and inventors, broadband is little more than a big, fat, fast, dull pipe. Broadband will fulfill its promise only if a new generation of inventors and thinkers and bright minds is determined to advance the cause. Happily, the groundwork is in place. Already, the engineers, capitalists, and investors who have devoted their energies to the vision of broadband are effectively creating a new alphabet—a toolset that can connect anyone, anytime, anywhere to anyone else. These tools will allow communications with organizations and our fellow human beings in a natural, intuitive fashion.

The beginning of the alphabet, the broadband infrastructure, is taking shape now. More than 40 million homes worldwide are connected to broadband, and the number is rising fast. With the groundwork being laid, the emerging need now is to inspire people to learn this new alphabet; to use the tools, and to bend and twist them into new shapes and forms and possibilities to fulfill the broadband destiny.

So what can this new alphabet do? What does it change? Why does it matter?

The truth is that few conditions of life, work, recreation, and family are untouched by broadband. In the 1980s, we wondered what we ever did before the fax. Now we wonder how we ever did without e-mail. Next, we'll marvel at how primitive we were before broadband. This is not to suggest broadband is somehow better, somehow innately superior, to its predecessor technologies. What broadband does, however, is produce more value from technologies that already exist by making it easier, faster, and more intuitive to use them.

Broadband changes the way people work, the way they learn, their relationships with family, what they do for fun, how they order take-out food, where they travel, whether they travel, the movies they watch, homework, electricity, sports, security, even the temperature inside their house. Broadband empowers individuals to make better decisions by making information more immediately accessible.

Beyond Dot.com

Despite broadband's dependence on the Internet as a source of consumer interest and economic nourishment, there's a distinction to be made between the two. It would be unfortunate if broadband were to be dismissed as just another form of the Internet. In particular, the differences between the broadband economic evolution and what is now derisively called the dot.com economy are important.

True, people living in the 40 million-plus households that have a broadband connection generally use it to accomplish the same sorts of things they previously accomplished using slower dialup access to the Internet. They read news articles from websites, they buy tickets to entertainment events, they bid on merchandise from eBay, they conduct school research, they send instant messages to friends, and they download files in order to play music, produce video clips or install new software.

But it is equally important to understand that the term broadband is not synonymous with web browsing or the Internet. Nor, within a few years, will broadband even be associated purely with personal computers.

It's simply that access to the Internet is the first logical application of broadband for two reasons. First, Internet access as people generally know it performs very well at speeds delivered by modern broadband networks. In fact, because the underlying comparison is usually a slow-moving dialup connection, broadband positively shines as an Internet access medium even at the bare minimum of 1 Mbps.

The second reason is economic. The willingness of millions of users to pay $40 or $50 per month for a higher-speed connection to the Internet creates the early source of funding for deployment of broadband services and the underlying infrastructures that deliver it. Without the Internet and the stunning demand it has generated among everyday citizens, it is doubtful that providers could justify the huge capital demands of provisioning their networks to deliver broadband. Dreams of an interactive, rich-media future are fine, but investors generally prefer solid evidence of payback schemes, consumer demand models, and returns on invested capital. Residential Internet demand is the early economic fuel for broadband; without it, broadband would be stuck in a digital media Catch-22 and this book would not be written today.

The capital investment required to make broadband data connectivity available at affordable rates to the average citizen has been mind-boggling. The U.S. cable TV industry has spent an estimated $70 billion from 1995 through 2002 to ready its fiber-optic and coaxial cable networks to support broadband services, including high-speed Internet access. Telephone companies have poured billions of additional capital into similar initiatives to lace their networks with souped-up digital delivery technology that transforms the telephone system from an instrument of voice communications to a medium of data.

Without a demonstrated appetite for high-speed data connectivity on a massive scale, cable and telephone companies would not have had access to the investment capital required to outfit their networks for broadband. Other than a general notion that people have a hearty appetite for content, and that digital delivery of content seems to be a sensible deployment approach going forward, there exists no ready application or service other than Internet access to justify such huge amounts of capital.

Yet the wellspring of demand for Internet connections among everyday citizens has proven to be exactly the tonic needed to jump-start capital investment in broadband. The simple math indicates that, with close to 20 million U.S. households hooked up to broadband connections and paying $40 or so a month for the privilege, broadband Internet access today is a huge business, generating $800 million a month, or roughly $9 billion a year, in consumer spending. That's an astonishing amount for a category that virtually did not exist five years ago.

So it is that the first mass-market application for broadband is faster access to the Internet. Reports from the front lines of cable and telephone providers suggest it is an appropriate application that delivers great consumer value. The presence of *churn*, or the tendency of customers to hook up, sample the service for a few months and disconnect, is negligible in the broadband Internet access model. Marketing executives who study churn and consumption patterns report that people like their broadband, and they're not willing to give it up. Even though some of broadband's truly magnificent applications have yet to arrive, the marriage of broadband data connectivity with today's Internet seems to work.

Erkki Liikanen, a member of the European Commission, notes that broadband connectivity and the Internet do get along nicely. "Widespread access to broadband carries powerful economic and social implications. Broadband will change the use of the Internet, by improving its quality, by making users enjoy rich content, applications and services, and by improving their productivity," he says.

That's certainly true. Yet to look at broadband merely as a way to render faster web-page access or to make it easier to zing off an e-mail message is to unduly limit the potential of the broadband platform.

Today's online providers already know this, and they're scrambling to remain relevant as broadband connections continue to grow fast. The tension between early arriving online service providers and the new world of broadband connectivity is dramatic. America Online (AOL), the Virginia-based giant of the online industry and the company that has introduced the concept of online communications to a vast swath of middle America, has raced to keep up as broadband connections displace AOL subscribers.

Often, the people who subscribe to new high-speed Internet access services provided by cable and telephone companies are the same people who got their first taste of online communications courtesy of AOL, which historically has dominated the dialup access market. At its peak, AOL delivered online service to more than 26 million U.S. households—nearly one of four homes on a given street. Yet many of them have been lured away, smitten by alternative online access provided through higher-speed brands delivered by cable and telephone companies. AOL executives have admitted as much. "We largely missed the first wave of broadband," said AOL chief executive Jon Miller at a December 2002 investor presentation. AOL is now embarking on new plans to remain the online service of choice in a broadband world and has introduced its own broadband service, AOL for Broadband, which features exclusive content and features.

This emigration of dialup loyalists to broadband shows how tastes are changing as broadband makes its steady encroachment into the incumbent world of dialup Internet access. For AOL, new service offerings, such as online voice-mail and exclusive video and music content, are designed to convince customers to stick with the service as they contemplate richer, faster broadband connections.

The AOL effort illustrates the evolving interplay between the old-style Internet access business and the emerging broadband marketplace. A corresponding observation is that even as key pillars of the dot.com economy were toppled during the "new economy" crash, the broadband march continued. From April 2001, when many believe the dot.com economic meltdown began, to December 2002, the U.S. broadband market tripled, rising to more than 15 million residential subscribers.

In fact, broadband never was synonymous with "dot.com" and the attendant hubris of that era. Nor are the spectacular flameouts associated with the dot.com sector reason to believe broadband is not real.

That one word—*hubris*—seems always to emerge in verbal autopsies of the late 1990s dot.com boom, whose ghosts include amusing but failed business ventures such as foofoo.com, a web-based retailer of high-end gifts, and Pets.com, whose infamous sock-puppet mascot is a poster child for e-commerce collapse. What began as fresh-faced enthusiasm about new ways to communicate, learn, and live ended in a chaotic tantrum of financial and industrial ruin. By some estimates, $1 trillion of equity contributed by investors was erased in the dot.com collapse. The two-headed ogre of greed and arrogance took what started as a good idea, and transmuted it into the reckless pursuit of individual wealth. It did so by promulgating hype that couldn't be substantiated.

In the life history of broadband, the Internet bubble of 1999 is Mardi Gras, and its financial ruins of 2001 and 2002 are the inevitable hangover.

But, the point is that the implosion of the dot.com bubble did not drag down broadband with it.

That's because broadband is not the Internet, but broadband does make the Internet faster and better. During and after the many nadirs of the dot.com frenzy, broadband Internet usage kept growing. By April of 2002, a report from the media measurement firm Nielsen//NetRatings showed that the majority of total time spent on the Internet came from people connected to broadband networks. That's saying a lot, given that there were still considerably fewer broadband Internet users in April of 2002 than there were traditional dialup users.

Summary

The twenty-first century is staring with a big bang of its own: broadband. Thanks to the high-speed, always-on network we call broadband, any person in today's electronic global village can access a bounty of content previously unimaginable—virtually anything, anywhere, anytime. Already, more than 40-million residences throughout the world are connected to broadband networks, enabling people to enjoy on-demand access to information that allows more informed decision-making than ever before. Broadband is about making each individual the center of universe rather than requiring people to travel to physical locations or be available at specified times to gain access to information.

CHAPTER 2

BROADBAND'S BIRTH

NETWORKS THAT ALLOW US to communicate thoughts, expressions, languages, ideas, and pictures across distances have been around for a long time. As early as the fourth century, B.C., people are believed to have employed crude forms of networking by shouting to one another from hilltops and towers with the aid of megaphones. In ancient Persia, messengers solved the limitations of voice by traveling on horseback to deliver information within a day from one city to the next. Over time, without wires, electricity, or circuits, humans developed increasingly clever ways to transmit messages across the land. By unleashing puffs of smoke up into the sky, native American Indians conveyed messages to their tribal brothers across distances greater than voices could travel. In the eighteenth century, the king of France employed a system of flags and beacons to transmit information between Paris and the city of Lille, on the country's border with Belgium. Relayed from various send-and-receive stations, it took 9 minutes for a simple message to make the 135-mile one-way trip; a more complex message, consisting of more complicated arrangements of flags, could take half an hour.

Contrast that system to today's emerging world of broadband. In March 2003, scientists at the Stanford Linear Accelerator Center were able to transfer 6.7 gigabytes of data (that's the equivalent of two movies on DVD) from Sunnyvale, California to Amsterdam, Netherlands in less than a minute. A collaborative effort by more than 170 United States universities, called Internet2, is working with private industries to construct a cross-country data backbone that will speed digital information along at 10 gigabits per second. The Internet2 project's goal is to leapfrog beyond today's data rates so that users can connect to one another at 100 Mbps. As previously noted, our opening broadband definition of 1 Mbps will fast become a rather humble standard.

Generally speaking, broadband owes its origins to a steady evolution in electronic networks that has brought us where we are today. Among broadband's forefathers is the telegraph system, which is essentially an electromagnet capable of communicating a coded alphabet by sending electronic pulses along a wire. In 1844, inventor Samuel Morse sent his infamously cryptic message, "What hath God wrought?" from a court chamber in the U.S. Capitol in Washington, D.C. to a receiving station in Baltimore nearly 40 miles away, and the fundamental elements of what would become today's broadband networks—physical transmission facilities and codes made of electronic pulses—were unleashed.

The telephone network, still a star performer on today's broadband stage, succeeded the telegraph in the late 1800s, a period of head-spinning invention. Brought to attention commercially by a near-obsessive inventor, Alexander Graham Bell, the telephone and its surrounding distribution network has since developed as a foundation of the world's most prevalent form of residential broadband—DSL. The telephone network remains the physical means by which a majority of residential computers connect to the Internet.

It was, in fact, an unplanned marriage of the computer with the telephone network that was responsible for introducing the world to the possibilities of digital telecommunications, the underpinning of broadband. The convenient fact that the telephone network is nearly universal, and that it uses a switching technology allowing any single user to connect with another, sets up the possibility for computers and their users to freely exchange information. Now, making good on that possibility is no mean feat; it has taken an incredible collaboration among governments, scientists, academicians, and industry to create an underlying scheme of standards-based rules and languages that have brought about today's Internet and a wide array of earlier data-networking technologies. Yet without an underlying firmament for connecting digital machines, the Internet, if it existed at all, would be purely a tool of the elite, rather than the mass medium it has become. The telephone network, which supplanted the telegraph, which supplanted the pony express, allowed the Internet to flourish as a consumer medium. It is a certainty that, in allowing the Internet to be born, the telephone network must now evolve into an instrument of broadband in order to survive.

Broadband's Building Blocks

Of course, our telephone networks won't be alone in their pursuit of broadband traffic. One of the levers of broadband's rapid growth is competition among networks for connecting people to broadband data. Today, a handful of robust networks deliver broadband to the home, and each has the effect of goading and evoking better performance, pricing, and availability of the others. No matter which of them ultimately wins the day, the reason there is even a battle at all has to do with a fortuitous convergence of two general information technology trends:

1   The digital revolution has enabled us to translate all sorts of information, including text, sound, pictures, and video, into digital code—the language used by computers. This digital revolution allows

you to see an image of the Mona Lisa over the Internet, hear an entire Led Zeppelin album archive from a set of digital compact discs, or watch a replay of tonight's top news story from a website maintained by CNN. Once transformed into the rather malleable language of digital messages, bits and pieces of content can be divided into manageable packets. These packets are sent through a communications channel and, miraculously, reassembled at the other end to recreate the original image, sound, or video clip. Further, the mathematics behind digital compression, or the ability to get rid of redundant information while preserving excellent reproduction, allow far more information to travel over a network than in the old days, where most information was transmitted in the far less efficient format known as analog.

2   The network revolution has changed the structure and workings of most of our familiar networks: from the telephone network to the cable television network to the computer networks of old. Now, rather than serving a single purpose—telephone networks were made for telephone calls, cable TV networks were meant to deliver television programs—networks have become multipurposed. Thanks to work that has occurred on the digital front, you can send computer files over the phone network, make phone calls over the cable TV network, and swap video images over the company's high-speed local-area network (LAN). Because the fundamental content is stored digitally—through an ingenious combination of 1s and 0s that make up computer code—the network doesn't care as much as it once did what you send over it, provided that the sending and receiving devices on either end can handle the new language of digital. Moreover, new schemes for building networks and ways to lay in new high-capacity technologies, such as optical fiber, have resulted in networks that are simply bigger, faster, and—most importantly—more affordable to average people than ever before.

Going Digital

We'll get to explanations of how broadband technology works in another chapter. But it's important to have at least a basic appreciation of the idea of digital technology as it relates to text, sounds, pictures, and video—the core content of broadband media.

Analog technology, which has historically been the dominant means of delivering content over networks, relies on a one-to-one relationship between the way content is captured or recorded and the way it's reproduced or played. For example, the tape recorder you fooled around with as a kid used a microphone on one end and a speaker on the other. The sound produced by your voice is captured as a stream of electrical fluctuations. This exact same pattern of fluctuations is passed through an amplifier and then to a speaker without alteration.

Digital technology, on the other hand, makes sounds (or reproduces text or pictures) by listening to (or sampling) the original output at a fast speed, and assigning a numeric code that represents what it heard. (The code is made up of groups of 1s and 0s; hence, the term *digital*.) This digital representation of the content can be passed through a network and fed to an analog converter that turns it back into the same sort of pulses and electrical fluctuations your analog recorder used in the first place.

Why bother with the entire arrangement of sampling, coding, and then decoding just to do what an analog instrument already does?

Two reasons. First, digital code is purely that: a code. If the output instrument can decipher the code, it can use it to reproduce the content that the code represents without disruption or degradation. That's why you hear so much about the quality of digital media. Movies that are correctly encoded on DVDs, for example, play back more crisply and cleanly than movies stored on videotapes (analog). As long as the code is intact, the video is reproduced with almost none of the degradation that haunts the analog media world.

Second, after content is represented purely by combinations of numbers, smart computation engines called *digital signal processors (DSPs)* can look for patterns within those numbers, and use those patterns to substantially compress duplicate information. That makes it possible to reduce dramatically the amount of electromagnetic spectrum or bandwidth required to carry digital content. It also makes digital networks highly efficient conduits of information. Broadband networks are digital in that they carry large amounts of digital code that represent various types of content. Data rates, such as 1 Mbps, measure how much digital information travels through a network per second.

It is worth noting that the concept behind digital networks has been around for centuries. The system of flags and beacons used in eighteenth-century France precedes today's digital network because it used symbols to represent spoken words.

The idea that we can zing computer information across electronic networks has long been proven beyond reproach. During the 1960s, airlines were among the first large industrial users of computer networks. Leasing dedicated phone lines, they developed an early online, shared-data network that allowed travel agents and reservationists to check fares and schedules and to book flight reservations. An obscure company, Carterfone, also deserves some credit for furthering the data-networking revolution. Its late-1960s battle to win regulatory approval to connect small portable radios to the AT&T telephone network ushered in an historic decision that cleared the way for a flood of new devices that could connect to the telephone network: answering machines, cordless phones, and, importantly, computer modems. Prior to the Carterfone approval, it was illegal to connect nontelephone devices to the U.S. telephone system.

Modems and More

A *modem* (the name comes from a coupling of modulation/demodulation) is a centerpiece of the broadband infrastructure. As the use of computers climbed in the early 1960s and beyond, a need arose for a device that could convert computer data into a language recognizable by the telephone network. AT&T's Bell 103 modem, which operated at a data rate of 300 bits per second (bps), was the first answer. Modems performed the neat trick of allowing computers (which speak a common language made up of digital code) to talk to each other over a telephone network that heretofore spoke a different language known as analog. Basically, the sending modem took digital information and translated it into a series of electrical tones that could be accommodated by phone lines. (Just like speech sent over telephone lines, the tones are audible and recognizable. They're the scratchy sounds that signal the connection of telephone modems.) The receiving modem heard the tones, recognized what they meant, and turned them back into their original language of digits, so they could be understood by another computer.

We have encountered a steady increase in modem technology ever since. In fact, broadband began as the next somewhat logical step in what has been a progressively faster data communications network: Sluggish 1200 bps telephone modems, in the mid-1980s, leapfrogged to 2400 bps in 1985, then to 4800 bps, then to 14.4 kilobits per second, and later to 28.8 kbps. Those phone modems, used initially to connect computers to bulletin boards and now the Internet, topped out at 56 kbps. The prevailing 56 k modem is likely to be as good as it gets in the world of analog modems, pressing both the laws of physics and the ability to keep up with changes in the telephone network itself. Newer cable modems, attached to cable television networks, and DSL modems for phone-line broadband, are now receiving the most investment and attention from manufacturers.

Faster Corporate Networks

Before exploring the development of DSL and cable modem technologies, a salute is owed to a separate piece of the data-networking puzzle. Around the time the residential world was becoming transfixed by the computer bulletin boards of the 1980s, or exploring proprietary online services such as Prodigy and CompuServe, a high-speed revolution already was afoot in corporate and government arenas.

By the mid-1980s, most large institutions were convinced of the productivity enhancements spawned by computers. Yet, there was a general recognition that the fruits of computing, such as faster computation and ready access to data, were not being unleashed across organizations as prolifically as they might be.

The answer would be rooted in experiments of the past two decades. Twenty years earlier, IBM had succeeded in building a nationwide network of interoperable computers that were connected to one another. The SAGE project, for Semi-Automatic Ground Environment, allowed the U.S. government's Department of Defense (DOD) to share data and computing power among banks of large mainframe systems. In the 1970s, the DOD furthered the computer networking model by developing protocols — a set of agreements about the treatment of data—allowing information to be shared among different kinds of computers. The protocols developed by the government, including a set of rules known as Transmission Control Protocol/Internet Protocol (TCP/IP), would emerge as a fundamental building block of today's Internet. Still, at the time, it was the ability to interconnect different brands and models of computers that broke new ground. That effort, coupled with IBM's willingness to make public its standards for connecting computers (cabling, protocols, and more) launched a new business category known as networked computing.

At Xerox Corp.'s notoriously inventive Palo Alto Research Center (PARC), a set of standards for computer networks was introduced in the early 1980s. Known as Ethernet, it combined hardware specifications, cabling configurations, interfaces, network architectures, and software specifications to yield the foundation for the modern office-computing network, known as a local-area network (LAN). Since then, it has been codified by the IEEE LAN/MAN Standards Committee, and has seen an increase in data rate to 10 Gbps from 10 Mbps.

The LAN swept like a storm across corporate and government institutions, delivering sharp productivity gains as more workers could share expensive printers and documents, and reports once imprisoned in a single workstation became available to any employee with security clearance and an inexpensive PC. Corporate networks, backed by large information technology funds, also delivered something most users hadn't experienced before in tinkering with early generation home PC modems: raw bandwidth. LANs could zing data from a basement server to a 20th-floor PC with astonishing speed; it seemed to users as if they were extracting data from their own internal hard disc rather than a machine located elsewhere.

Some of the early efforts in residential broadband communications were inspired by the LAN, and many of them employed—and continue to rely on—the fundamental building blocks of office computing. Ethernet interfaces, for example, allow home computers and appliances to be connected to broadband networks. The first commercially deployed cable modem technology came from a company (mine, as it happens) whose name paid homage to the predecessor technology of the corporate computing world. We called it LANcity.

Today, the kind of computing power and bandwidth once known only to large institutions is available to home users at affordable prices through a handful of technologies. Two of them, telephone-based DSL and cable television's so-called cable modem service, currently dominate the worldwide market for residential broadband and should continue to be the main conduits for broadband for the next five years until they, too, are supplanted or at least enhanced by other technologies, such as optical-fiber networks that snake their way to the home. Telephone-based DSL and cable modem technologies, however, are the first to bring broadband to the home because of an inherent efficiency: both use an existing infrastructure to deliver broadband connections. Rather than rewire entire nations with enormously expensive information networks (as was envisioned in the early 1990s), we have managed to coax new tricks out of the existing cable TV and telephone networks. Briefly, here is a history of how that happened.

History of DSL

Across the world, telephone wires once viewed solely as instruments for carrying a human voice from one sending device to another receiving device have morphed into high-speed, multimedia circuits.

Unlike what is tenderly known as *POTS*, for *plain old telephone service*, the telephone network has grown to encompass a last-mile transmission capability that is rooted in something known as ISDN, or Integrated Digital Services Network, lines. DSL, the popular broadband transmission service, is an offshoot of ISDN, which uses existing telephone wiring to deliver a digital signal across the access, or edge, portion of the network that serves individual homes.

DSL technology turns the historical telephone network into a high-speed broadband delivery instrument. In a way, DSL has revived a maturing business—that of using the telephone network to carry phone calls.

DSL's roots trace back to the early 1960s, when digital communications technology was introduced to improve performance of the core portions of the telephone network used to transmit long-distance calls. In basic networking topologies, the business of getting signals where they're supposed to go has historically involved amplifying the signal; that is, boosting its energy level and compensating for a gradual reduction in energy as it hurtles down the pipe. Without amplification, telephone calls would become inaudible by the time they reached their destination. But there's a trade-off. Amplifiers are unable to distinguish between the signal they're supposed to maintain and the unwanted background noise that is introduced along the network by a host of associated electronics. With each boost supplied by an amplifier, noise, too, is amplified, potentially to the point where it reduces the desired transmission to a mess of unwanted interference. Think of what it sounds like when you attempt to tune your AM radio to a distant station. Enter digital. The problem that digital overcomes is one of noise. By using the magic of digital coding to create an exact replica of the desired signal at designated points along the network, a virtually perfect, noise-free transmission is assured (at least until the signal reverts to amplified analog form deeper in the network).

The telephone network consists of a series of signal-processing locations called central offices that are connected by high-capacity trunk lines. From these central offices sprouts the vast labyrinth of twisted-pair wire that ends up at a phone jack inside your home. That collection of wire and associated electronics, called the local loop, is the telephone version of the so-called "last mile" of connectivity that has become a central feature of broadband communications. Only recently, with DSL technologies becoming widely available, is the final segment of the telephone network beginning to pulse with digital data. But within the interoffice phone network—that is, the various central offices and the larger toll offices that support them—digital is old news. Much of this traffic had been converted to digital by the 1970s as long-distance traffic, corporate data, and mammoth switching machinery chugged along a high-capacity digital conduit. Thus socialized to the wonders of digital signal transmission in the network core, the telephone industry began to explore further implementation of digital down into the busiest tendrils of the network, where millions of residences and business were connected via tiny twisted wires. The exploration wasn't easy. It wasn't until 15 years later, with the first market trials of ISDN technology in 1985, that the local loop changed from purely an analog implementation to a hybrid affair. Most people who use the telephone network purely to make phone calls or to hook up low-speed computer modems are making use only of the analog functionality of the local loop. But with ISDN and its successor technology, DSL, phone calls and voice calls can travel at the same time over the same thin copper wire; a byproduct of the efficiency of digital data.

Bringing ISDN technology to bear throughout the telephone network required an immense effort lasting more than a decade, consuming billions of dollars of capital and yielding a service that, unfortunately, seemed to be too little, too late. The ISDN specification, built to deliver digital data at the now-unimpressive rate of 128 kbps, presumed a world of brief data sessions, relatively slow transmission speeds, and support primarily for digital phone calls. Alas, none wound up being particularly suited for the Internet, which scarcely existed as a consumer medium at the time of ISDN's introduction, but looms now as the central force behind the broadband revolution.

The disappointment over ISDN wouldn't last long. A different breed of ISDN service, DSL, would emerge as the telephone industry's shining star in the digital universe and, at least as of this writing, as the world's most prevalent means of broadband connectivity.

Serious exploration of DSL technologies began in the mid-1980s, as captains of the telephone industry took notice of increasing demand for high-capacity digital connections known as T1 and E1 lines. Once envisioned purely as means for interconnecting telephone central offices, T1s were being ordered up in substantial number by businesses that wanted reliable, high-speed private lines to shuttle files, messages, and data over wide geographies. A market was emerging, and a U.S. telephone industry roiled by the 1984 breakup of the Bell system knew it.

At the telephone industry research and development facilities Bellcore and AT&T's Bell Laboratories, work was under way to develop an easy-to-implement networking technology that would work within the engineering structures of the existing phone network. T1 lines were expensive, and customers often waited weeks for installation. Overcoming those twin concerns would mean re-engineering a simplified version of ISDN that could be overlayed more easily onto the existing local loop, and delivered at a fraction of the cost of T1 lines. The key, and an early driver of the first commercial version of DSL known as high-data-rate digital subscriber line (HDSL), was to eliminate the need for costly and cantankerous signal-repeaters required by T1 lines. That, and other engineering feats designed to assure acceptable error-loss levels and maintain signal reliability, went into the brew that would become HDSL. By 1997, more than 450,000 HDSL lines were in service worldwide, and the technology of DSL was in business.

Still, HDSL costs were out of reach for the mass market. By the early 1990s, a competitive threat to the world's largest phone system was looming on the horizon. Both factors would figure in the development of a new DSL variation that would take hold with the consumer populace.

In the early part of the decade, federal regulators in the U.S. began chipping away steadily at laws and rules protecting the local telephone monopoly. At the same time, the cable television industry, which had grown from its 1940s inception into a formidable media powerhouse, had completed wiring the nation with high-capacity networks capable of transmitting more than just TV channels. War seemed inevitable between the two camps as cable companies flirted publicly with the idea of providing telephone service, and telephone companies spoke just as brashly of infiltrating the world of wired cable TV services.

A Video Vision

In fact, the onset of the modern DSL age owes much to efforts by the telephone industry to develop a transmission technology not for the purpose of broadband Internet and data distribution, but for sending commercial-free movies to residential customers in direct competition to cable TV. In 1994, a beaming Ray Smith, then chair of the regional phone company Bell Atlantic, gushed with pride about a new technology called Asymmetrical Digital Subscriber Line (ADSL) that would revolutionize the way Americans got their television service. "I've seen the pictures," Smith was quoted as saying in press reports as he introduced the technology, "and they look gorgeous." Smith's company was one of three large telephone firms that had joined together in a venture called Tele-TV. The mission, as described by lead evangelist Bell Atlantic: to generate $4 billion annually within five years through new video dial-tone services that would make movies, TV shows, and events available to millions of subscribers.

In fact, the venture never got beyond a limited, 1000-home trial that took place in Fairfax County, Virginia, from 1995 through 1996. There, a Tele-TV service branded Stargazer made use of the upstart ADSL technology to deliver digitized movies like *Pulp Fiction* and TV shows like *Saturday Night Live* to viewers who could order, pause, rewind, and fast-forward at will. Based on a downstream, or to-the-home delivery rate of 1.5 Mbps, Stargazer proved that ADSL would adequately serve good-quality video over the existing telephone network. (ADSL is labeled as such because of a speed imbalance: It provides the high downstream rates needed to stream video and fast Internet access, but features a slimmer, slower upstream path.) The ADSL concept has since been sanctioned by the American National Standards Institute, which christened the technology as standard T1.413.

Following the demise of Tele-TV, the cable and telephone industries ultimately ratcheted down the level of war rhetoric, and the concept of video dial-tone hasn't been heard of since. Nor, except in a few scattered instances, has DSL emerged as a favored means of distributing television channels and programs.

Yet the prophecy of Ray Smith and leaders of the telephone industry did come true in a way. A technology invented as a means of competing with cable television proved to be a worthy adversary. It's just that the battleground came to revolve around the Internet, not television. Since Bell Atlantic made its video foray in 1995, the Internet has swelled in popularity. As ubiquitous as the Internet might seem now, it's instructive to recall how head-spinning and utterly new things seemed in the early- to mid-1990s. The creation of the World Wide Web gave users access to millions of pages of information and entertainment. People were buying computers and connecting to services, such as America Online, in record numbers. Millions of pages were being added to the web monthly. Portals sprang to life. Companies developed electronic commerce applications. If your company didn't have an Internet strategy, it was considered a dinosaur.

Suddenly, the same DSL technology that had been shelved by the telephone companies had a new purpose: providing high-speed transport of data files over those very same copper telephone lines. By connecting local lines to digital send-and-receive equipment, DSL delivers plenty of room to allow for both voice/phone/fax calls and high-speed broadband digital data. Normal telephone conversations travel through a relatively Spartan amount of spectrum (0 to 4 kHz, to be exact). Downstream data (from the central office to the home) ride along frequencies ranging from 200 to 1000 MHz. And upstream data (home to central office and beyond) are assigned the 20- to 140-kHz frequencies. With DSL's frequency-allocation model, it's possible to deliver substantial bandwidth even over the thin wires that already weave their way into millions of homes.

Act of Faith

DSL's climb to prominence was hastened both by increasing demand for a better, faster Internet experience, and changes in regulations designed to put more competition into the telecommunications system. The most notable of these regulatory changes was the passage of the Telecommunications Act of 1996 by the U.S. Congress. A sweeping piece of legislation, the Telecom Act was billed as a sort of fuel-injection of telecommunications competition. After massive lobbying assaults by industrial agents on all sides, it basically came down to the following bargain: U.S. telephone companies could finally enter the assumedly lucrative long-distance market in exchange for allowing local rivals to connect their equipment to the existing local loop, and deliver services over the very same lines maintained by the incumbent phone companies.

If the logic behind the Act—to invite newcomers to make money over the facilities of their main rival—seemed flawed, nobody argued much when a slew of investment followed. Rather than concentrate on the slow-growth market for voice services, rivals focused on the rising demand for corporate and residential data, and they seized on the newly invented DSL technology as their ideal enabler. Overnight, or so it seemed, a dozen or more independent DSL providers rented office space, raised billions in capital, and came knocking on the doors of incumbent phone companies seeking the keys to the central office, where they staked out floor space and set up racks of DSL equipment. Companies including Covad Communications, Rhythms Netconnections, DSLNet, Northpoint Communications, and others stormed the market, each of them bearing a new acronym: CLEC, for Competitive Local Exchange Carrier.

The Telecom Act gave rise to these and a massive number of new local carriers. Before the Telecom Act became the law of the land in 1996, there were, by one count, fewer than 100 local carriers in existence. That number mushroomed to 230 companies vying for consumer and business dollars in 2000. Handsomely funded by private and public money, these upstarts invaded the territories of the well-known and well-heeled incumbent local telephone companies and became engaged in a battle to wrest away their best customers by offering lower prices, better service, or both.

These competitive interlopers probably deserve the most credit for jump-starting the deployment of broadband services over the nation's ubiquitous copper telephone wires. After they were given access to an incumbent's network, they weren't satisfied with simply reselling traditional voice services. They were seeking a service that would differentiate them. They literally built their business plans around the new high-speed Internet access technology known as DSL.

Thanks to the wherewithal of the CLECs and the eager investors that backed them, a fury of activity and effort had been unleashed to make DSL part of mainstream USA. Positive results came about immediately. New, internationally endorsed DSL technical standards helped vendors manufacture more efficiently and in greater volume the microprocessors, modulators, and modems necessary to outfit the phone network for DSL service. Costs for the technology plummeted as demand spiraled. Cheaper chipsets and central office gear helped spark DSL deployment outside the U.S., too, as international telephone companies took advantage of the favorable economic conditions spawned in part by the U.S. legislation. DSL penetration in aggressive-deployment countries such as South Korea, Hong Kong, Taiwan, Canada, and Belgium quickly surpassed U.S. levels. By 2001, South Korea and Hong Kong boasted more than 3.5 DSL lines for every 100 citizens, more than triple the 1:100 ratio in the U.S.

Still, even in the U.S., DSL providers were nearly overwhelmed by demand as the Internet's popularity soared and online users yearned for a better, faster Internet experience. Backlogs of tens of thousands of orders were common for national DSL providers.

Yet the party didn't last. Relationships between CLECs and incumbent telephone companies, or ILECs, were strained from the start. It often took weeks for an ILEC to turn over a single DSL line to a competitor. Some charged incredibly high fees to the CLEC to place the necessary equipment in the central office. Then, they made it so costly for CLECs to buy the line that there was virtually no profit margin available, unless the CLEC overcharged its customers. At first, this strained relationship had little effect because investors rewarded the CLECs based on the number of subscribers they could attract. That resulted in a land grab not seen since the Old West pioneering days. But in 2000, the economic landscape changed dramatically, and the CLECs were a high-profile victim. The larger CLECs, nearly to a one, have crumbled under the pressure of overcapacity, frustrations in securing access agreements with incumbent telephone companies, and tremendous competitive pressure both from cable TV companies and from the same telephone companies that were ordered by the government to open up their facilities.

Telecom stocks, which led the stock market boom of the late 1990s, have since generated losses on paper believed to total more than $1 trillion. Investors simply poured too much money into too many companies that, essentially, were building the same networks. "The market was getting drunk on the juice we were drinking," the Federal Communications Commission chair Michael Powell told the *New Yorker* magazine in late 2002. "There's no question, we went too soon too fast. Too many companies took on too much debt too fast before the market really had a product, or a business model."

Still, the technology of DSL has thrived even as the underlying structure of the telecommunications landscape has been badly shaken. When the Telecom Act became law, there were fewer than 50,000 DSL lines in the U.S. Today, there are believed to be more than five million DSL households in the U.S., and more than seven million DSL customers in North America at large. Even after several highly publicized flameouts of would-be DSL providers, such as Rhythms Netconnections, DSL is going strong. Worldwide, it remains the most prolific of the broadband networks. In the U.S., where the DSL revolution began, the leading providers of DSL service today aren't newcomers, but the old standbys—the regional phone companies that own and operate their own lines. BellSouth, the most aggressive of the U.S. telephone companies, tripled its number of DSL subscribers in 2001.

As the telephone companies' priorities changed from providing video to a more data-centric and Internet-based model, several different forms of DSL technology have been developed. In fact, the list is now so long it reads like a complex alphabet-soup of choices and options. For example, there's symmetrical DSL, which provides an equal amount of bandwidth in both the upstream and downstream directions. SDSL, which starts at 192 kbps and goes up to 1.1 Mbps, is primarily aimed at business customers who need to receive and send large files.

Work continues to improve DSL technology by extending its reach and by making it faster and cheaper. For example, an emerging European standard is based on technology that would boost speeds to 2.3 Mbps in both directions. Others are working to send signals beyond the 18,000-foot limitation that exists because DSL signals degrade over distance, limiting access to customers located outside that ring.

In many ways, the creation of DSL technology has transformed our notions of what the telephone network can do. DSL has turned a decades-old network into a fast-moving broadband conduit. Few have been quite so poetic in describing the transformation of telephony into a residential broadband instrument as the chair of

British Telecom, Sir Christopher Bland. "Our copper wires have lain in their ducts or hung from their poles for up to 40 years," he said. "And for decades they carried nothing but phone calls. They were simply 'talking wires.' With the advent of the mass market Internet in the '90s, the wires started to sing a little. And now, the broadband Internet promises to transform these same lines into entertainment highways. In other words, the wires are starting to dance."

History of Cable Modems

In the early 1990s, when the world was just beginning to awaken to the possibilities of digital communications, when the Internet was a tool not of 15-year-olds with web browsers but serious academicians with hulking mainframe computers, a team of enthusiastic engineers were inventing a way to shuttle digital communication streams—the stuff of today's Internet, e-mail, and more—through a new type of "pipe."

This pipe was built, oddly enough, not to deliver e-mail messages and route web pages on request, but to carry television signals. Channels such as Home Box Office, ESPN, and CNN coursed through its high-capacity wires and optical tentacles to a box connected to your television set. It was cable television, of course. Tens of thousands of miles of what the industry called *plant*, or the physical network of coaxial and fiber-optic cables mounted on wooden utility poles and laced through underground conduits, had been constructed over the last 40 years or so for the single purpose of getting more television to your living room. It worked. Thanks to cable television, by the early 1990s, nearly seven out of ten U.S. homes had access to 60, 70, 80, or more different television channels. The industry ran to big, powerful broadcast networks like ABC, CBS, and NBC, was a $15 billion media titan. Born in the U.S., cable television has migrated to other places; today, cable systems are pumping out dozens and even hundreds of TV channels across every continent.

But beginning in the late-1980s, forward-thinking inventors were interested in cable TV for a different reason than just television. It was a time when the concept of computer networks had taken a firm foothold throughout corporate and institutional America. Large organizations had proven that by removing the desktop PC from its isolated berth and making it part of a bigger, more capable collective, they could accomplish some amazing things. Information that once was hidden from view inside one person's machine could be shared, even enhanced, by many users. Documents were released from the prisons of dusty library shelves and published for all to see. Communications changed overnight. Networking protocols—essentially the rules of behavior, etiquette, and language that allowed one computer to talk to another—

became codified and widespread and standardized, and as they did, they proliferated. These rules, which went by names such as Novell and Ethernet, became prominent within corporations and institutions, giving rise to the term *local-area network (LAN)*.

Many engineers and inventors who had marveled at these new tools of communications wondered about ways to translate what was going on inside of companies and organizations to a wider geography. What if they could take information stored inside the mainframe computer of a school building, for example, and make it available to another classroom across town? Instead of a local network, there would be a metropolitan network, able to zoom documents, images, and more. (In an attempt to do just that, in 1990, with the support of my colleague and mentor, Bill Elfer, I formed LANcity.) But it was apparent that to build a metropolitan-area network would require a transmission medium, or a physical foundation, over which the information could move. The existing telephone network was a dense labyrinth of copper wires that lacked the pure transmission speed enjoyed by corporate LANs, which used thick cables that could carry more information, faster. DSL hadn't been proven commercially as a broadband data medium. Speedy transmissions were available over a souped-up version of the telephone system, going by names such as T1 and T3 and ISDN, but they were prohibitively expensive.

Happily, the same sorts of cables used for corporate LANs—coaxial cables—had already been buried and strung all across town by the local cable television company. They could, with a bit of tinkering and some careful engineering, serve as a powerful medium of transmission for data communications—the very sort of instrument that, at the time, lots of companies and institutions were demanding. Businesses, schools, hospitals, and municipal agencies wanted ways to transfer computer files, images, and all manner of written and visual materials across town, or even within their buildings, quickly and efficiently. Many built their own pipes, and some rented expensive slices of extra capacity from the local phone company.

But others couldn't shake the notion that a perfectly capable delivery medium—or perhaps even a superior, faster delivery medium—was literally right outside the door. The cable television industry had built, in some ways, an accidental network. A sleek, fast, multibillion dollar data network that was brought up to believe it was a television medium but seemed suspiciously well-suited for data.

It took several years of toil and persistence, and not a small amount of capital, but ultimately the cable television network would be transformed. LANcity invented the foundation technology for what would become the first so-called "cable modems," or the boxes that, attached to a cable TV system, could transform cable from a medium of television to a medium of digital data. As many had hoped, its speed and its affordability were remarkable. In a perfectly happy coincidence, around the time it was launched, a new force in consumer media began to grip the world. It was called the

Internet. Coupled with the cable modem technology that was developed, originally, to help businesses and institutions zap files around the office, the Internet's arrival ushered in a new generation of high-speed, connected households.

The road to cable data services has been a long one. As with most useful technologies, cable modems carry an iterative, storied past. They predate the World Wide Web itself—by at least two decades—although the early models would be hard to pick out of a lineup of 1980s-era metal electronics boxes.

For starters, cable modems of yore were bigger than what lines the shelves of today's electronics stores. Much bigger: The size of a toaster, in many cases. They weren't sleekly packaged for residential ambiance because they weren't meant for homes. They were meant for offices, schools, fire stations, city and county buildings—in short, institutions—not homes.

Also, they were used differently. The Internet, at the time, was a complex linking of universities, government facilities, and sundry technologists. Its communicative abilities were mostly dispersed through electronic bulletin boards, with clunky access methods, over very slow, dialup phone lines. These were the monochromatic days of orange or green type on black screens; when PCs were toddlers, and their operating systems immature; when system crashes and inscrutable technical jargon gave rise, sadly, to rampant PC phobia—"I don't want to touch it, I'm afraid I'll ruin something." (It was the DOS days, for those who remember. Not Windows. Not yet.) The Internet had no World Wide Web. It was great for hobbyists and technologists; it was not suitable for most everyone else.

Cable's Metamorphosis

In these days, if PCs were babies, the cable-television business was in its early 30s. A city-to-city sprint in the 1970s to snatch up city-granted franchises, or the rights to string wires and lay cable across the metropolis, had subsided. Dozens of loosely regionalized cable systems existed. Most cable channel lineups topped out at a capacity of 50 channels. Attracting more subscriptions to basic cable services, and luring existing cable customers toward premium channels, such as HBO and Showtime, was the industry's consuming focus.

Cable plant and its basic architecture was also different 20 years ago than it is today. The use of fiber optics—a given today—to shore up transmission lines, reduce the proliferation of noise-inducing amplifiers, and increase reliability was still hotly debated. (There were people who thought fiber latched to coaxial cable would never work.)

Cable systems started, then, and still now, with a headend, which is like the central nervous system, where TV pictures were collected from over-the-air broadcasts (ABC,

CBS, NBC) and from satellite (cable channels such as CNN, TNT, the Discovery Channel, and many more.)

At the headend, pictures and sound were captured and placed into an organized channel lineup, then launched out onto miles of coaxial cable, toward homes. Five times or so per mile, the signal would need a boost by an amplifier. But here, as with the telephone network, boosting the signal meant boosting any noise, too. The more amplifiers strung up like Christmas lights, one after the other, the worse the picture at the end of the line.

The topology of the 1980s cable network was tree-and-branch: Fat cables stretched, north, south, east, and west, from the headend to drop-off points, where thinner cable branched out into neighborhoods. From there, one more branching off, to subscribing homes. It was a one-way architecture that did an adequate job of sending lots of TV channels to lots of viewers. But it was in no way suited for the task of data communications, for a variety of reasons.

One of them—probably the key failing at the time—was that cable-television systems could send signals in only one direction: from a central location to a subscriber's home. They lacked a means to send signals in the reverse direction, or back up the network *from* the home. In order to work for data transmission, there would have to be a way for users to send data back up the pipe, back through the headend, and out to a wider network where they could find their ultimate destination, be it another computer address, or, later, a World Wide Web site.

The vast majority of cable systems in the 1980s hadn't begun lighting up the path from subscribing homes back to headends—called the *upstream path* or the *reverse path*, in contemporary lingo—because there wasn't enough user demand to warrant the investment. But that didn't stop developers from marveling at the sheer carrying capacity of a coaxial cable network, and thinking about ways to harness the industry's bandwidth for more than merely video delivery. It would take an enormous effort to rebuild the cable industry's networks to support two-way communications. But it would also require the invention of a new class of electronics devices that could marry the stuff of data communications technology with the wires, amplifiers, and headend architectures of a modern cable system. Cable had big, fat pipes. It needed a special class of data modems, however, to begin its transformation into a data network.

The cable modem of the 1980s wasn't even called a cable modem. Because it was designed and used primarily by engineers, who tend to be succinct, it was just called a modem, or sometimes, an RF modem, where the RF means radio frequency. It *mod*ulated (imprinted information), and *dem*odulated (extracted imprinted information). The information was digital—1s and 0s—not video, and it moved on the carriers of the frequencies already contained within the cable's spectral boundaries.

Early cable modems served various purposes. Some cable providers agreed, as part of franchise negotiations with a given city, to link up various city buildings—the firehouse, police department, libraries, schools—with what was called an institutional network, or I-net. With an I-net, the attached buildings could send rudimentary messages to one another over a protected swath of the cable system's existing plant. Unlike today's speedy devices, though, cable modems at the time topped out at about 19.2 kbps. This was blazingly fast compared to dial-up telephone modems of the same timeframe, which crawled along at a feeble 1200 bps, but head-shakingly quaint by today's multi-megabit-per-second standards.

Early cable modems were decidedly less complex, and, as usually correlates, less sophisticated, than today's devices. A message from a connected building was sent from a PC, attached to the toaster-sized modem, upstream to the cable headend. There, the message was simply handed to the designated, protected downstream frequency, without any processing, and was broadcast to all connected buildings. The recipient building received the message through its toaster-sized modem. So did everyone else, but their equipment didn't "see" it, because its address didn't correlate. It was the electronic equivalent of writing a note to one person, and applying this logic: I'll assume everyone is John, and send the message to everyone. But because nobody else is uniquely John, he's the only one who will see to receive it.

The cable-television companies themselves recognized the innate, communicative abilities of the plant they'd built, and they made use of early cable modems for their own internal communicating. Headends aren't always near a telephone line. In fact, they're often located in remote, hard-to-reach areas: the tops of mountains or amid miles of fields. Rather than pay the local telephone company to run a line to a remote headend, why not use modems on either end of the cable lines, already strung? So went the logic. It was the early style RF modem that let cable engineers rig up these internal PBX systems. Great grandparents to these units are still used today for residential telephone service.

Where there's phone, there's data (and vice versa). Soon, engineers figured out a cable modem that could latch T1 speed (1.544 Mbps) data communications over cable plant. They used it to offer leased T1 services to businesses, but there was a hitch: Each company that wanted a T1 line used the equivalent of one full television channel, and few cable operators at the time had vacant channels available. Far be it for a thinking cable company to displace the popular HBO, or ESPN, for a private data network that would serve a few office buildings.

Thus, despite the early success indicators, the cable modem would sustain a 15-year wait before it became mainstream. Three difficult realities confronted pioneers in the field. First was a copious lack of two-way plant, needed to move information from homes to headends as well as it could in the other, broadcast direction. It wouldn't be until the late-1990s that the majority of U.S. cable systems were activated for bidirectional signaling, an absolute prerequisite for true high-speed Internet services.

The second obstacle was the niggling matter of a business model. Activating I-nets kept city fathers happy, true. But on the books, it looked unpleasantly like an all-cost, no-revenue endeavor. Ditto for internal communications. Something was needed that would propel the cable modem into the residential marketplace — the cable-television industry's lifeblood.

The third hurdle to overcome was the equipment itself. In many cases, it was custom built for a particular application. In all cases, it was proprietary to each individual supplier, and certainly not interoperable. That meant that cable companies risked putting their investment in a technology that might be usurped, and quickly supplanted, by a rival method. It meant that the modems sitting in one warehouse and intended for a particular market might not work two communities away. The president of Continental Cablevision, Bill Schleyer, was particularly persistent in raising these questions. The answer ultimately would come in the form of DOCSIS — the Data Over Cable Service Interface Specification penned and trademarked by the cable industry's not-for-profit research and development arm, Cable Television Laboratories Inc., in 1997. DOCSIS was an immediate shot-in-the-arm to the development of cable modems on a more economical, volume-driven foundation. But until then, it was a supplier's market: What they had is what cable providers got.

Bicoastal "Eureka!"

There were a few cries of "Eureka!" along the way to interoperable modem technology, or the ability to use the same modem purchased in California with a cable system in Maine, or anywhere else. They occurred across the U.S. geography, from California to Massachusetts to Philadelphia, in the early 1990s.

One happened in the corporate hamlet of Pleasanton, California, then headquarters to Viacom Cable (a company since sold to Tele-Communications Inc., and later, acquired by Comcast Corp. of Philadelphia). As the story goes, Viacom's director of technology development, Doug Semon, a current member of the CableLabs DOCSIS Certification Board (and a hopeless gadget-head, having built himself a computer long before there were computers), happened upon a cable modem in 1993. It was made by a company known as Hybrid Network Technologies, a nearby Silicon Valley neighbor. Semon was smitten by its applicability as an Internet access device for hobbyists. He noted, too, that the cable modem contained a built-in telephone modem — handy for those cable systems not yet upgraded for bidirectional (two-way) signaling. Semon began to muse about its possibilities. The first thing that came to mind was a more socially significant, and potentially more useful, application of the cable system than the industry-standard local franchise giveaway known as a *public-access channel.*

A requisite of most government-awarded franchises, the public access channel was a standard television channel made available, although usually sparingly used, for local civic groups and schools to produce video programs. Instead, Semon mused, a cable modem installed in schools and libraries could greatly improve the research resources available to students.

Semon won approval from his supervisors to launch a trial project. He proceeded with a series of modem tests, still working with Hybrid. Early one afternoon, an executive with Hybrid called, agitated, insisting on an immediate meeting. Semon climbed into his car and headed to Cupertino, wondering what on earth was going on. Inside the company's office, the Hybrid executive typed from his keyboard a long string of letters and numbers, starting with "http://www." Using a pre-Netscape, Mosaic-brand browser, available in prototype form only, the two reached out over the Internet to a graphically oriented page, stored on a computer server physically located in Germany. It was one of six known websites on the planet at the time.

Semon rushed back to Pleasanton to describe the significance of what he'd seen to Viacom Cable's president, John Goddard. The Internet, empowered with a graphical interface and called the World Wide Web, looked intriguing. With a consumer-friendly tool, now known as a web browser, it had the makings of the missing ingredient in the quest for a two-way cable architecture: consumer demand. A residential, cable-delivered service that was a good deal faster than dialup methods could be the economic driver the cable industry had been seeking. Previous experience showed that Americans prefer more to better—witness the huge percentage of VCRs set to extended play to record every possible bit of tape, at the cost of better resolution. Americans would probably also prefer faster (cable modem) to slower (dialup phone modem).

A trial ensued, in 1994, to 50 homes in Viacom's Castro Valley, California system, which had already been upgraded for two-way signaling because of a previous interactive television experiment. Hybrid was joined by Intel Corp. and General Instrument Corp. (now owned by Motorola) to provide equipment. The modems sent data downstream (to homes) at a rate of 10 Mbps; upstream information ran at 128 kbps. The state of the art in telephone modems, at the time, was 28.8 kbps.

The results were almost too astounding; consumer acceptance was almost too high. Relying purely on word-of-mouth marketing, Viacom nursed a backlog of some 200 eager subscribers who wanted to be part of the trial. Phrases were coined: "It changed my life," originated by a Chinese subscriber who couldn't regularly contact his family, in China, without his cable modem. "To get this cable modem back, you'll have to pry it from my cold, dead fingers": origin unknown, but widely circulated in industry circles to this day.

Similar revelations were occurring across the cable television industry, in places like Cambridge, Massachusetts, where Continental Cablevision was putting early generations of cable modems to the test. Dave Fellows, a veteran cable engineering executive who was among the first to explore the data-over-cable connection, recalls Continental's efforts in Cambridge, where the cable company charged its first users $100 a month for a residential Internet link.

"By September of 1994, Continental had wired the entire campus of Boston College to the Internet with LANcity modems, offering Internet access in every dorm room on campus," said Fellows.

"I believe the longest, continuously connected-over-cable site is the Cambridge Public Library."

Cable modem trials and deployments were beginning to build across more companies, and more markets, some involving early-day predecessors of modern Internet service providers such as Prodigy and CompuServe. In Philadelphia, where executives with Comcast Corp. also applauded the notion of a Hybrid/Intel/GI modem, Comcast put the gear to work in 50 trial homes within the company's nearby Lower Merion, PA system. The system was picked for its demographics: More than 60 percent of Comcast's Lower Merion customers owned a PC.

In all cases, the cable modems weren't cheap. Each ran upwards of $500. Without standards, scale economics were difficult. Without standards, no single manufacturer might enjoy the rosy promise of high-production volume, and the development of robust competition—a huge influence in driving down prices—was unlikely to come about.

Yet cable companies believed they were on to something. Not since the introduction of pay television services, such as Home Box Office, in the late 1970s had cable companies enjoyed the sudden boom of incremental business that some saw looming in the form of high-speed data communications. One by one, major cable operating companies rushed to explore the boundaries of this potential new application for their medium. Beginning a multi-billion dollar wave of capital investment that would continue for years, they began raising funds to rebuild their cable systems for a data dawn most believed was now at hand.

DOCSIS Is Born

By the mid-1990s, two of the three coagulants that had gummed the adoption of cable modems 15 years earlier had, for the most part, been dissolved. Activation of the upstream, home-to-headend path was a perfunctory part of cable system upgrades, coast to coast. The ebullient results from Cambridge, Castro Valley, and Lower Merion were spawning enthusiasm from other cable providers to learn more about the technology, consumer acceptance, and business models.

Matters also looked good for cable modems on a macro, telecommunications business level. The Internet was on the rise. The cable and telephone industries, which for the better part of 1990-1994 had been arming for a battle to snitch each other's core businesses—the telcos readying residential video service, cable readying residential phone service—put their weapons aside. That mutual retreat, coupled with the rise of the World Wide Web, afforded a nearly perfect environment to nurture a fledgling new business: extremely high-speed Internet access, using cable modems.

Only one barrier remained: equipment interoperability. Without a standard, cable modems would never be interoperable. It was more than an arcane technology concern. Without interoperability, a thriving market for cable modems was unlikely to emerge. For one thing, modem developers were loathe to commit to huge manufacturing volumes if they feared their proprietary techniques might be sideswiped by unforeseeable technology developments. If volume remained slight, prices would remain high—another concern related to consumers.

It was common, even expected, that most consumer electronics equipment would work properly no matter where its user resided. Without interoperable modems, a customer might purchase a whiz-bang cable modem in Tulsa, Oklahoma, only to find it incompatible, and thus useless, when he moved to a suburb served by a different cable television company. If you've ever navigated a confusing array of electrical power outlet incompatibility while traveling abroad, you have a sense of the sour possibility. And retailers, obviously, would never support, or sell, a technology that threatened to spawn angry customers who were burned by incompatibility issues.

Interoperability issues revolved around numerous technology choices that early developers were confronting. Some suppliers made asymmetrical modems, meaning that more information moved more quickly to homes, than from homes. The reasoning: Sending a click to retrieve a web page requires considerably less bandwidth than the page itself.

Other suppliers, including LANcity, were making symmetrical equipment, believing that as broadband activities increased, residential users would want more upstream speed and girth.

As the enthusiasm for cable-delivered, high-speed Internet grew, so did the list of cable modem suppliers, each with a slightly different way of going about it. It was less a case of "one size fits all," and more a case of "all sizes fit many." And the supplier list was growing. Big-name suppliers entered the scene: 3Com, Cisco Systems, Hewlett-Packard Corp., IBM, Motorola, Northern Telecom, and Zenith.

Smaller suppliers—Com21, LANcity, and Terayon, among others—started to tremble a bit, seeing the specter of big manufacturing ready to stamp out modems like cookies, one after the other, for prices much more attractive than they could offer. It was a market share sprint, where everyone moved as quickly as possible in a non-standardized, proprietary environment. Standards, in 1995, were the mantra: Everyone endorsed standards, provided that the standard centered on their technology. (When that didn't work out as intended, from the viewpoint of some of the larger players, such as H-P and IBM, they retreated from the scene.)

In those days—1995—standards were largely a new concern for the cable industry, at least as it related to in-home electronics. During the 1990s, cable had outfitted its headends, plant, and subscribing homes with equipment made by a short list of manufacturers. It made for an innately tense coexistence for both suppliers and cable providers. The lead suppliers held most of the control over pricing and features; namely, when the former would go down, and when the latter would get included.

By late 1995, a small group of cable technologists began to meet privately to discuss a clandestine silicon chip made by a clandestine, Silicon Valley company called MicroUnity. The chip, unlike every chip used up until then, was completely programmable. That meant the chip could be put inside set-tops and cable modems and later be updated with applications as they changed. The alternative was the status quo: new service, new box. New boxes, for cable providers, carry steep capital and operations expenses. There's the extra cost of the box itself, and then there's the cost to send someone out to install it, known in the lingo as a *truck roll*.

The cable technologists—leaders from Tele-Communications Inc., Time Warner Cable, Comcast Cable, and Cox Communications—thought enough of MicroUnity's programmable silicon idea to both invest in it, and form a private holding company that would steer its use in cable hardware. They called the company MCNS, which stands for Multimedia Cable Network System.

As the discussions matured, it became clear that the driving motivator for MCNS was to attract more hardware suppliers into the cable business, and to be released from the perceived pricing and features stranglehold of the industry's big suppliers. The only way to go about it was to insist on interoperability among cable equipment providers. The only way to garner interoperability was to develop a standard.

Enter CableLabs, the Colorado-based research and development arm of the cable television industry. What started as MCNS soon became the Data Over Cable Service Interface Specification, or DOCSIS (pronounced dock-sis). Realizing the strategic importance of cable modems and high-speed Internet services, CableLabs, in November 1996, put the project on fast-track status, girding to have a complete specification written by the end of the year.

By mid-1997, the specification was ready to undergo lab tests of prototype DOCSIS gear at CableLabs. The intent was to provide an ongoing incubator for the vendor community, to sample and test the specification.

In September 1997, CableLabs released a detailed certification program, and formed a Certification Board to review, and ultimately approve, products that met the DOCSIS specifications. It was decided that makers of the headend part of high-speed cable Internet systems, known as Cable Modem Termination Systems (CMTS), would be tested to *qualify* with the specification, and makers of cable modems would be tested to be certified, for which they received a DOCSIS-certified sticker.

Certification Begins

Two years and three certification test waves would transpire before any vendors' products became DOCSIS-certified. On that fateful day—March 20, 1999—Cisco Systems received qualification for its CMTS. The first certified cable modems came from Toshiba and Thomson Consumer Electronics. A month later, modems made by 3Com, General Instrument, and Arris Interactive passed certification, and in ensuing months, dozens of products made the DOCSIS cut. To this day, many of those who follow broadband's development credit the cable industry's speedy effort to rally around a common standard as the key reason why cable companies currently lead DSL in the U.S. broadband deployment race.

Meanwhile, success stories about cable modems and high-speed Internet services continued to accrue. So-called early adopters were literally lining up for cable modems. The industry itself was thrilled to satisfy the demand, for reasons that went beyond pure economics. In the 1990s, the cable industry's perception as the poster child for poor customer service was at its peak. (Remember the less-than-flattering 1996 movie, *The Cable Guy*?) Everybody likes some positive attention, sometimes. Water-cooler talk elicited smiling stories of truck chasers, ordinary citizens who ran after cable trucks, arms waving, to beg for cable modem service.

Across the nation, in rollouts of high-speed Internet service, consumer demand far outstretched the supply of technicians who could install the service. (At the time, two were needed: one to handle the cable modem, and one to handle the PC.)

Business models were emerging, some quite dramatic. In Palo Alto, California, the local cable provider, a cooperative known as the Palo Alto Cable Co-Op, sampled the high-end pricing range—and it worked. Reasoning that Pacific Bell (now SBC Communications) charged between $200-$1000/month for ISDN and T1 service, the cable co-op debuted a three-tier pricing card for its high-speed cable modem service: $99/month, $399/month, and $599/month. It immediately signed 60 customers, and vowed that data revenues would exceed video revenues by 2001.

By the end of 1998, the North American cable industry counted 550,000 cable modem subscribers. That grew to 1.6 million by the end of 1999 and five million a year later. At the end of 2002, there were more than 16 million. Over the same time span, the cost of cable modems has declined steadily, from $500 or more in the mid-1990s, to the low $120 range by summer of 2001. The sheer enormity of DOCSIS, and its speed to adoption, is an indisputable success story. The momentum behind cable's new data delivery business spawned entire new companies including Time Warner's RoadRunner high-speed cable modem service, and the much-celebrated but short-lived @Home Corp., a collaboration among investment bankers and several large cable companies. @Home built a sprawling backbone network and an entire service and content infrastructure to support the newborn cable Internet category. The high-flying, high-profile Silicon Valley company ultimately was destroyed by infighting with its partners and the inability to continue service agreements with the cable companies that once supported it. But in its brief history, it provided a jump-start that allowed the cable industry to grab a dominant market share of the broadband residential marketplace.

DOCSIS itself has continued to develop. Cable modem circuitry is now available on slide-in, PC cards, on chips built right into PCs, and in Europe, it's inside set-top cable TV boxes that are connected to TV sets. The successor version, DOCSIS 1.1, folds in the ability to deliver quality-of-service standards that support the next generation of broadband services. These will go beyond mere Internet data to span such services as digital telephony and true video that's layered over a two-way, DOCSIS-paved Internet Protocol path.

In the unfolding story of broadband, cable television has fashioned for itself a prominent role. And DOCSIS can honorably be immortalized as its true beginning.

Summary

1980s corporate and office environment networking breakthroughs proved the enormous value of high-speed networking at the workplace, opening up new opportunities for productivity and for participation in global commerce. DOCSIS-compliant cable modem and DSL standards were not even on the drawing board then, but broadband's fundamental building blocks were emerging. Modems were getting faster, content was getting digitized, and personal computers were becoming faster and cheaper than anyone expected. Cable television and telephone networks that were built for different purposes until then were suddenly in an excellent position to take the advantages of this revolution—and ultimately empower individuals with broadband to the home. A race began between the cable and telephone industries to hook up millions of customers to new high-speed two-way connections. It continues today, even as engineers work behind-the-scenes to invent new services that will ride along the high-speed broadband conduit.

CHAPTER 3

THE BROADBAND BAZAAR

A BROADBAND NETWORK has one purpose: to move massive amounts of information, swiftly and reliably, from one place to another, making the information available anywhere and at any time. The bigger the information, the better suited it is for broadband versus narrowband networks. Video, for example, is big, relative to audio or text messages, and performs much better over broadband.

Nonetheless, information can be an on-demand television show, a digital encyclopedia, a music file, a telephone call—anything that can be digitized and, if necessary to fit into the distribution medium, compressed—assuredly including services that have yet to be conceived.

After all, if humans could speak loudly enough to be heard from coast to coast, and over oceans, or if we had eyes keen enough to see those distances, we'd have fewer reasons for interconnected communications networks.

But we don't.

Basically, broadband involves a sender or information source, a recipient, and a fast, reliable, and secure means to link the two in a way that lets them interact. Today, those reliable means are in place in the form of cable television, telephone, and wireless broadband networks that solve the once-vexing problem of how to deliver broadband data rates directly to residential users.

Behind the Last Mile

For most consumers of broadband services, the experience is defined by the amount and type of activity that occurs in the portion of the network that's closest to them—the so-called "last mile." Known in industry parlance as the *access network*, it is loosely defined as the section of the communication system that branches off the last routing device and connects to the home or business desktop.

The access network has generally been the slowest and most congested element of the broadband network at large. It is also the area of the network that gets the most attention because it's where innovation is taking place and where new technologies are being developed to deliver greater speed and to improve the broadband experience. Cable television and DSL networks are the primary examples of last-mile broadband connectivity today.

Notably, the access network is also the portion that's most populated with devices. Today, that includes personal computers, PDAs, security cameras, and televisions. Tomorrow, it might include telephones, refrigerators, security alarms, and heating/cooling systems, among other things.

Behind this access network lies what is known as the *backbone*. The backbone is a place where seemingly infinite amounts of data packets zoom around the planet, riding along fiber-optic and copper-based roadways at incredibly high speeds as they course their way to and from devices that speak a special language called Internet Protocol (IP). It is an incredibly complex web of crisscrossing highways that ultimately enables users to enjoy the benefits of high-speed broadband services.

The term backbone evokes images of a spine and ribs—or a centralized system consisting of a main artery and hundreds of branches that lead off in every direction to the outermost reaches of the planet. That image is not only too simplistic, it is also inaccurate. Instead, the Internet backbone should be thought of as a huge net that covers the globe in a mesh-like grid, with intelligence and control mechanisms distributed in myriad locations along the way.

This web-like architecture, in fact, is what gives the Internet its "fail-safe" feature—back when the Internet was first devised, it was designed to allow government officials and agencies to communicate in times of conflict or disaster, even when one or more regional centers of communication was disabled. The idea was to distribute intelligence throughout the network and provide redundant signal paths as a way to keep the network up and running.

Ultimately, however, it is this network core, or backbone, that determines the upper limit of any broadband experience. Much like the urban highways of today, the Internet backbone must be constantly monitored, maintained, and upgraded to allow for an ever-growing amount of traffic to merge onto it. When traffic grows to a level where it's being choked and doesn't flow freely, additional capacity has to be provided.

That means if you're trying to download a video or an audio file from the web, the speed of that download is dictated first by the backbone capacity, then by the speed and capacity of the access network.

Remember that the Internet is not a monolithic, uniform network. It is truly a network of networks owned by different companies. Therefore, there is no singular backbone; in fact, there are several. At last count, there were more than two dozen such backbones of varying sizes and capacities operating in the United States alone. Owned by such recognizable companies as AT&T, Uunet, Cable and Wireless, and others, these networks carry packets of data that represent voice, video, and data across state, country, and international borders. This is possible because network owners have developed and agreed to business relationships with their peers, allowing them to exchange data.

In the years before the dot.com implosion, it was fashionable for service providers to actually build their own backbones, primarily because they wanted to be able to tout their ability to control their customers' experiences. A side benefit came from the fact that they could sell excess capacity to other Internet service providers and large businesses that needed to transport data to and from several locations. However, the exercise was expensive, and not well coordinated. Soon, there was more global capacity than was needed for the traffic that was being generated.

Today, a state-of-the-art backbone consists of hundreds of fiber-optic strands, each of which can carry a dizzying amount of traffic. Certain portions of the backbone—including the links between highly populated areas such as New York and Washington, D.C.—have been upgraded to the point where each fiber can carry multiple channels of traffic, with each channel having a capacity of 2.5 gigabits per second (Gbps). That's more than enough capacity to send e-mail, surf the World Wide Web, and even watch streaming video.

But as broadband services gain in popularity and traffic on the Internet grows to include movies, videoconferences, and other bandwidth-hungry services, these backbones have to continue to grow in capacity, be partitioned accordingly, or be re-engineered to include new routing techniques so they're not choked with traffic. Imagine what would happen today if several hundred thousand, or even millions, of people wanted to access a movie that's debuting over the Internet. That volume of requests, combined with the size of the files being sent, would choke the backbone even before it got to the access network, which has even less capacity.

Backbones today are linked via fiber optics instead of copper wires. Fiber networks cost about the same to build as copper-based networks, but are practically limitless in the amount of bandwidth they offer. Signals can travel farther over fiber-based networks without being amplified, and they suffer much less degradation when compared to traditional wire-based networks. For this reason, as time goes on, fiber will continue its slow march toward the home, possibly reaching the doorstep at some point in the future when traffic levels and economics justify it.

A Spectrum of Possibility

Whether we're talking about last mile or backbone, behind any telecommunications network is a product of the physical world. The *electromagnetic spectrum* is an array of frequencies, which include everything from radio frequencies to microwave, infrared, gamma, and ultraviolet light. Through engineering principles that themselves would (and do) occupy entire books, it's possible to attach information to these invisible electromagnetic lanes so that the information can be carried from place to place.

continues

Broadband networks use assigned allocations of frequencies to handle their high-speed digital data traffic. The frequency allocation for broadband data over DSL networks, for example, is 5 kHz to 1 mHz. Effectively, these are the "lanes" of the electromagnetic spectrum over which digital information travels in the DSL world.

Cable television networks divvy up their available spectrum—measured in gigabits per second—another way. Although invisible to cable television customers, a well-orchestrated division of traffic occurs within the confines of the physical fiber-optic lines and cables that snake their way to the home. Assignments vary a bit among North American, Asian, and European cable systems, but the following scheme, typical in North America, offers a simple guide to what goes where:

- **5–42 MHz**—Upstream communications used by two-way, interactive services. A click from your mouse to request a web page travels over these frequencies.

- **50–550 MHz**—Downstream analog services, such as traditional TV channels. When you watch CNN, for example, you're most likely consorting with the 50–550 MHz band.

- **550–860 MHz**—Downstream digital services, such as digital video, telephony, and data.

Variations in frequency usage do exist between cable providers, but this example is a good general depiction of how cable providers divvy up the spectrum that they built their networks to harness. These assignments are not set in stone. Even today, cable providers discuss taking the large swath of spectrum currently devoted to analog cable channels and converting it wholesale to digital traffic, thereby freeing up enormous amounts of reclaimed bandwidth.

How Data Get There

Perhaps the easiest way to describe how information moves over a broadband network is to use a specific example. Let's say Scott, a guy who uses a cable modem in Denver, sends an e-mail to his boss, Bill, in New York.

In practice, the item that's being moved over the network could also be a telephone call, or a streaming movie, or a web page. After all, as engineers like to say: bits are bits.

First, Scott in Denver composes the e-mail, just like any other e-mail, and presses Send. The message itself exists in neatly defined packets—individual vessels carrying the contents of the e-mail message—and these packets are in turn organized into neatly defined frames that constitute the language of Ethernet. *Ethernet* is a common language and set of physical configurations for moving data from one machine to another.

When Scott's cable modem sees that it has mail to send, it raises a flag to indicate it has traffic and states the size of the traffic. The flag is intended for a companion unit, called a *Cable Modem Termination System (CMTS)*. The CMTS is generally located at a signal collection point, commonly known as the cable *headend*.

The CMTS is much like an air traffic controller: It constantly surveys the frequencies it manages within the overall cable plant, as well as all cable modems connected to it. Its job is to assure that data keep moving, in an orderly fashion, to and from its family of cable modems and the Internet itself.

The packets containing Scott's e-mail exit the cable modem, and travel in a portion of the electromagnetic spectrum that is specific to upstream (away from the home) cable networks. Specifically, that spectral zone resides between 5–42 MHz. (See the sidebar, "A Spectrum of Possibility.")

Scott's packets are attached to these upstream frequencies through a process called *modulation*. Modulation is a series of techniques that imprint information onto a communications carrier—itself an electromagnetic wave—so that the information can get to its destination.

On cable broadband networks, in the upstream direction, a type of modulation called Quadrature Phase Shift Key (QPSK) is commonly used. It is identical to the type of modulation used by satellite providers to transmit information to Earth.

QPSK is inherently sturdy and resilient against noise and interference, which is important in upstream signal transmissions because that spectral zone, between 5–42 MHz, can be fraught with interference from such intruders as CB radio, ham radio, and International AM signals. Put another way, it's slower than downstream modulation, but more impervious to bumps in the road.

NOTE   Later versions of the broadband specification known as Data Over Cable Service Interface Specification (DOCSIS), apply more advanced forms of modulation, which increase the speed and resilience of the upstream signal path. But the majority of deployed cable modems, as of early 2003, use QPSK modulation.

At some point in the upstream ride, Scott's packets shift off of coaxial cable, and onto a fiber-optic line, at a location called a node. From there, they ride a beam of light to the headend.

At the headend, Scott's e-mail moves into the CMTS, using the parameters specified in the DOCSIS specification. The CMTS already knows the distance between it and Scott's cable modem—it established and locked down that information when

Scott's modem was installed. It knows the distance of all other cable modems connected to it, too.

The CMTS readies Scott's packets to speak the language of the Internet, known as TCP/IP (Transmission Control Protocol/Internet Protocol). Having done that, the CMTS forwards the packets—essentially stamping them with information about where they're from (Scott's machine) and where they're going (Bill's machine).

Then, the packets that make up Scott's e-mail blast out into the Internet, transiting toward their destination address. Along the way, the packets might disassemble and ride completely different routes, and move through a series of other routers. Because the Internet was originally developed by the Department of Defense, a principle design criterion was to assure that messages got to their destination safely—which meant breaking them up and sending them along different routes, in case one route was damaged.

At the server that delivers Bill's e-mail to him, Scott's packets are reassembled, and placed into Bill's e-mail box.

When Bill replies, and presses Send, the same thing happens, in reverse:

1   Bill's cable modem raises a flag, indicating it has a message to send.

2   The packets, comprising Bill's e-mail, and speaking Ethernet, move into the upstream signal path, using DOCSIS mechanisms.

3   The packets get modulated with QPSK, for the coaxial portion of the ride; then get bounced onto a fiber optic line to the headend.

4   The packets move through the CMTS, speaking TCP/IP, through the Internet's routers to Scott's mail server.

5   When Bill's response moves onward to Scott's modem, the packets are imprinted onto a downstream carrier using a type of modulation called Quadrature Amplitude Modulation (QAM).

QAM is faster than QPSK—much faster—but less impervious to noise. However, the downstream spectrum used by cable operators (between 50–860 MHz) is inherently less prone to noise.

That's the essential sequence that occurs when bits of information travel along the broadband network (in this case a DOCSIS-compliant cable broadband network). With variations in modulation techniques and frequency assignments, the same sort of ritual is at work within other flavors of broadband, such as DSL and wireless high-speed networks.

Cable Modems and Networks

The preceding section traced the path of an e-mail message as a way to visualize the basic workings of a broadband communications network. This section delves into the workings bounded by the cable modem and the CMTS—or, everything that happens before the green light illuminates on a typical, residential cable modem.

Let's say we're still talking about Scott, and he just brought his cable modem home from the store. The paragraphs that follow describe what happened when Scott's cable technician came by to turn the cable modem on and get it working.

After the cable modem was connected to the coaxial outlet near Scott's desk, which itself was connected to the cable plant and the remotely located CMTS, the cable modem began scanning the downstream frequencies (50–860 MHz) available to it. Specifically, the device scans for a downstream channel modulated with QAM.

Many of the QAM channels seen by Scott's cable modem in that initial channel acquisition sequence are intended for the television set-top box in the living room. They contain digital video channels, not broadband Internet data. So, the modem keeps scanning this sea of digital data. Eventually, it locks on to a QAM channel. It knows to do so because the packets within that channel have a unique identifier, specific to all cable modems. In techno-speak, the unique identifier is known as a Packet Identifier (PID). Inside this PID are Ethernet frames destined for an address associated uniquely with a particular cable modem. In analogy, the unique identifier is a sorting mechanism: all greens over here, all blues next, all yellows over there.

After Scott's modem finds its downstream channel, it begins to make note of three key indicators being broadcast by the CMTS at all times:

- Time stamp, necessary for synchronizing its specific distance from the modem
- Parameters of the modem's upstream communications channel
- Upstream bandwidth map

Next, a ranging process begins. Because each cable modem is located at a unique distance from the CMTS, each modem's settings are unique. The settings include the time synchronization, transmission frequency, and power level for each transmission. Iteratively, over two or three tries, the CMTS fiddles with the cable modem, making adjustments so that Scott's modem is correctly timed, is sending information over the right frequencies, and isn't talking too loudly.

As soon as Scott's modem is behaving in a manner that is clearly observable and acceptable to the CMTS, it requests an IP address. All devices connected to a broadband network have an IP address—it is the origination or destination address of just about everything that can occur on the Internet. The modem gets its address from an item called a Dynamic Host Configuration Protocol (DHCP) server.

Now, Scott's modem is set up for transmissions and has a unique IP address. The last thing it does, before the green "ready" light turns on, is to download its configuration settings. Generally, configuration settings relate to the business rules of the broadband service provider. For example, a specific modem might be capped at no more than 3 Mbps of downstream bandwidth and 256 kbps of upstream bandwidth. Or, it might be allowed to perform both broadband Internet and voice services.

This entire process—ranging to acquire a downstream channel, upstream parameters, and IP address—occurs in seconds, if nothing goes wrong. When the process is complete, a light illuminates on the cable modem, indicating that it's ready for broadband.

It is important to note that the inner workings of the cable modem are a constant work in progress. Since the first cable modems were developed, the DOCSIS specification emerged to assure equipment interoperability—a fancy way of saying the modem you purchase in Toronto will work at your new home in California.

Since DOCSIS, which initially came out as DOCSIS 1.0, further advancements have materialized. DOCSIS 1.1 adds ways to tier broadband Internet services, and it shores up signal and data security; DOCSIS 2.0 brings a new form of modulation, which makes upstream signals move as much than three times faster as the original DOCSIS. Continued improvement on the specification, and on cable modems in general, is expected, especially as broadband services mature. Even so, the DOCSIS specification family is backward-compatible, meaning older DOCSIS modems continue to work even as enhancements are made to newer generations.

DSL Modems and Networks

In a series of U.S. television advertisements produced by Pacific Bell in 2000-2001, tension mounted as neighbors who receive broadband service from the local cable system see their data rates diminish with every new connection on the street. Once-friendly neighbors become sworn enemies, sneaking around with spray paint to single out "bandwidth hogs" who are siphoning off more than their fair share of broadband capacity.

The ads were a witty attack on what DSL proponents perceive as cable's Achilles heel: Hybrid fiber-coax (HFC) architectures, like those prevalent within the cable industry, are configured to share bandwidth among 500 or more homes served by the same signal-distribution node. The assumption is that cable's shared architecture causes insufferable bog-downs for cable modem customers as more and more users are added to the node. With DSL, the logic goes, customers don't have bog-downs.

As is usually the case, especially with funny ads rooted in exaggeration, the truth about bandwidth sharing lies somewhere in the middle.

The workings of a DSL network are loosely as follows: Homes with telephone service already are connected by twisted pairs of wire to a telephone facility known as a central office that is typically no more than three miles away. With DSL, a pair of modems are added to the existing connection; one at the home, another at the central office.

There, any voice conversation that was happening on the part of the phone line spectrally segmented for telephone service heads over to the phone switch. The data traffic, which rode in on a different spectral area of the same phone wire, enters a Digital Subscriber Line Access Multiplexer (DSLAM). Telephone companies use DSLAMs because the alternative—dedicating a router port to each individual DSL subscriber—would be too expensive. Something was needed for router port sharing, which led to the creation of DSLAM.

Multiplex generally means to cram, as in, cramming many inputs into one output. In this case, packing multiple DSL data flows into one port of a DSLAM.

Multiplexing is also a sharing mechanism. It doesn't matter much when subscriber levels remain low, because fewer people are sharing the DLSAM port. Sharing-related bog-downs are less likely to occur. That's partly why it is easy to dismiss potential sharing bottlenecks at the DSLAM: They don't tend to occur in the early life of a DSL customer.

But as overall DSL subscriber counts continue to rise, two things happen.

First, more traffic hurtles through the DSLAM. However, the Internet's language, TCP/IP, mitigates data overloads by tossing off packets, such that they have to be resent. First come, first served. (This is true for cable's broadband networks, too.) This all happens transparently to the person surfing away, but its symptom is slowness.

The second thing that can happen when DSL penetrations rise is lesser known. It's called *crosstalk* and is specific to twisted-pair wires that telephone companies use to deliver phone and DSL service. It is, of course, true that telephone companies run sets of twisted-pair wires to each individual home. Yet, those individual wires are, at some point higher up in the neighborhood network, bundled together into a single sheath, for linkage to the central office.

However, when phone wires are bundled together into one sheath to the central office, they're physically close enough that the DSL traffic, because of where it occurs in the RF spectrum, can radiate from one pair of wires to the next resulting in crosstalk. To the DSL equipment, crosstalk looks like noise. Sluggishness in the movement of data is its symptom.

This entire discussion might sound combative. As an early innovator of the cable modem, I suppose I contain a natural leaning toward the cable side of the competition between cable and DSL modems. It's true, and more than a little exciting, that the telephone industry has plenty of interesting technological approaches available to it, many of which could give new shape to the level of competition between both industries.

Indeed, the reader should know that a fine and respectable fight is gearing up between the cable and telephone industries. It's a good fight, and worthy of observation because it will benefit consumers. The fight will involve increasing levels of bandwidth, and making that bandwidth available for services that are increasingly enriching.

Understanding Shared Architectures

Understanding the impact of cable's shared architecture on broadband Internet customers starts with something called a node. Let's say 500 homes are clumped together on a node, which is the rule of thumb in the cable industry. Next, apply an expected customer penetration rate for broadband Internet service. If we assume the rate is 20 percent, that's 100 cable modem customers.

A network that is segmented into nodes, such as cable's HFC networks, necessarily means that available bandwidth, no matter how vast, is shared among customers.

Next, we estimate how many cable modems are online and working at the exact same time. For the purposes of this discussion, we'll set it at 40 percent. We're now down to 40 people sharing 27 Mbps in the downstream direction (toward customers). Evenly distributed, that's 675 kbps, or just over half of 1 Mbps each.

It doesn't stop there. Architecturally, most cable operators group four to eight nodes into service groups, which share an upstream laser transmitter and CMTS port.

When broadband Internet subscription levels rise, cable operators can immediately do two things to ease the pressure on the network. First, they can break up the number of nodes in the service group, to give each node more bandwidth.

Second, they can break the nodes themselves into fewer users—into node sizes of 250 homes, 100 homes, or even 50, for example, instead of 500. Both techniques are affordable, relatively fast ways to give more bandwidth to customers, before the impacts of sharing show up as bog-downs.

Wireless Broadband

Most of the discussion about today's last-mile broadband networks revolves around the two kingpins of the category: cable television and DSL networks. Together, they account for more than 90 percent of the world's residential broadband customers.

But an emerging alternative known as *wireless broadband* is worth note.

The term wireless broadband has grown several flavors over the past two years. The old-fashioned kind, known industrially as Multichannel Multipoint Distribution Services (MMDS), was developed as a way to send cable TV services to homes, without using wires.

This technology, which is especially useful in rural areas where the construction of physical, wired plant is excessive, has gone through several lifetimes of financial struggle. Nonetheless, some providers of wireless high-speed data remain, at this writing. Sprint Corp.'s residential broadband wireless services, for example, use MMDS techniques.

Wireless broadband also includes the nascent category of satellite-to-home data service. Satellites do a remarkably efficient job of sending data streams from a central point (a satellite hovering 22,300 miles above the earth) to multiple receiving points within a broad geographic range.

The residential high-speed Internet access service delivered by the popular U.S. satellite television provider DirecTV, for example, showers users with data rates of up to 500 kbps. The problem to date is one of symmetry, or in this case, the lack thereof. There is no demonstrated commercial model for a way to harness the power of satellite technology for an upstream path. In other words, users of satellite broadband services enjoy fast downstream delivery of web pages, streaming media, and more, but are relegated to slow dialup connections for outbound traffic.

DirecTV and others have sought to mitigate this problem by teaming up with DSL providers in a sort of hybrid solution: You get your downstream broadband from satellite, and you send your upstream signals via DSL. Savvy consumers recognize, though, that this hybrid scheme involves paying two separate fees to two separate carriers, potentially doubling or at least surpassing the normal expenditure for two-way broadband connectivity.

Efforts are under way to develop true symmetrical broadband-via-satellite, using high-powered satellites known as *Ka-band satellites*, but likely won't be a commercial force until at least 2005. Meanwhile, only a small fraction of the 45 to 50 million residential broadband households in the world receives service from satellite.

Then, there is the increasingly ubiquitous *Wi-Fi*, which variously refers to hot spots of bandwidth, available to laptop computers equipped with wireless network cards that are based on the IEEE 802.11 wireless/LAN standards. At the time of this writing, Wi-Fi hot spots are on a wildfire-like spread through coffee shops, hotels, and airport lounges throughout the United States and Canada.

Another option, *residential Wi-Fi*—which is the use of a wireless router inside the home—allows customers to share cable modem or DSL bandwidth among connected devices. Most U.S.-based cable operators are putting together or already offering wireless options to their broadband Internet customers, sometimes for a monthly fee that includes ongoing maintenance. (Anyone who has ever set up a wireless home router, at least in the early days of the technology, knows how time consuming it is to be the "MIS guy" of the house, or worse, the neighborhood.)

In both cases—Wi-Fi hotspots and residential Wi-Fi—the underlying technology is known as 802.11, which is usually followed by a letter: 802.11a, 802.11b, 802.11g, and so on. The letters indicate the particulars of what is offered over the antenna. 802.11a runs between 6–54 Mbps on 8 to 12 channels in the 5-gigahertz (GHz) zone, and can reach about 66 feet.802.11b runs between 2–11 Mbps on three channels in the 2.4-GHz range, with around a 330-foot maximum range. 802.11g offers speeds up to 54 Mbps, also in the 2.4-GHz zone, but with assorted types of modulation to fend off interference.

More wireless techniques are assuredly headed for the broadband marketplace, again to supply the growing level of consumer electronics gadgetry and advanced broadband services. It isn't hard to imagine where things are going, particularly with the large and increasing array of handheld devices. A portable, handheld display equipped with a tiny but voluminous hard drive and a wireless receiver, designed to store TV programs for viewing on the airplane, doesn't seem that far away. Already, cellular telephones are doubling as still cameras. Each year, at the annual Consumer Electronics Show in Las Vegas, manufacturers trot out more examples of new gadgets that can only get better with broadband.

The broadband angle in all this is the notion of a residential gateway, outfitted with high bandwidth wireless spigots. A bandwidth gusher connected to a wireless gusher, which slakes the thirstier and thirstier fleet of consumer gizmos. Wireless is destined to become more prominent in the broadband world, but its success depends in part on development of stronger security solutions than have so far been brought to market.

The OSI Stack

A communications network wouldn't work well if its various equipment partici-pants, invariably involving a wide range of suppliers, didn't follow a similar set of trans-mission rules. That's why the International Standards Organization developed a framework for everything that can happen to a traveling unit of information. It's known as the OSI stack, where OSI stands for Open Systems Interconnection. The point of it is consistency and equipment interoperability. The OSI stack contains seven layers, with each layer setting boundaries around its own objective and purpose. Broadband access networks, such as DSL and cable modem, are generally specific Layer 1 and Layer 2 technologies. The seven layers of the OSI reference model are as follows:

Layer 1	Physical layer
Layer 2	Data link layer
Layer 3	Network layer
Layer 4	Transport layer
Layer 5	Session layer
Layer 6	Presentation layer
Layer 7	Applications layer

Data moving over broadband networks is generally confined to the bottom two layers of the OSI stack.

The physical layer describes the modulation and error correction used over the access network plant. The data link layer, one level up from the physical layer, describes the languages used to move data to and from broadband users.

Home Networks: The Last Link

As broadband services have proliferated and won favor with their users, people have become eager to share that capability with other computers and devices in their house. Estimates suggest that as many as 30 million homes in the United States have multiple computers in them. Just as consumers have connected multiple television receivers to their cable TV lines, a single broadband connection can be shared among several devices via a network within the home. This allows a user to do myriad things, including: share printers and other peripherals; play games with other users; and share files such as images or spreadsheets. Going forward, home networks are likely to serve television and audio feeds, too.

Home-based networks operate in the same manner as the last-mile access network, but on a smaller scale. A router-type device is placed in the home and connected to the broadband network. End devices—whether they're today's personal computer or tomorrow's Internet-enabled kitchen appliance—have to be configured to speak the language of the Internet. These devices announce themselves to the router when they're connected, and the router recognizes the devices and enables them to communicate with the rest of the network.

The biggest differentiator between home networks is how the in-home devices connect to the router or access point. Two general options are using wires, or installing the increasingly popular wireless network.

Wires are perhaps the most reliable way to stay connected to the network, and several wire-based networks are available to consumers. Each device can be linked to the in-home router via specialized data cables, but that requires that the cables be put under the carpet, tacked to the walls and around doorways, or snaked behind walls to avoid an unsightly mess or damaging those cables by stepping on them, placing furniture on them, and so on.

Another option is to use the same coaxial cable that cable TV and satellite signals ride on throughout the house. This approach is great if the cable outlet is conveniently located somewhere near the computer or other device—which is not always the case. For example, it's probably a safe bet that there is a cable TV outlet in the media room, but there might not be one in the study or home office.

Other emerging technologies allow a broadband user to take advantage of either the existing telephone or electric wires to distribute broadband signals and avoid having to run new wires throughout the home. These approaches use various methods to place the data on frequencies different than the voice or electrical signals. That keeps them from interfering with phone calls or being disrupted by electrical noise that's created whenever household appliances are turned on. Older power-line technologies were known to suffer slowdowns in communication speeds as large appliances, such as clothes washers, dryers, and air conditioning units were activated.

Phone-line networking, most commonly referred to as HomePNA, is based on the specifications developed by a group of companies known as the Home Phone Networking Alliance. The group's original version of the standard operated at just 1 Mbps, but the second-generation specification operates at a much speedier 10 Mbps. The downside of HPNA is akin to the coax problem—if no phone jack already exists near the broadband device, one needs to be installed.

Any of these wired scenarios can be made to work, but the most popular option is to go wireless. In a wireless network, all of the computers in the home broadcast their information to one another using radio signals. This can make networking easy and a lot simpler to move computers around—an important consideration for laptop users and even more important in the future as other appliances become broadband-enabled.

Three types of wireless networks, ranging from slow and inexpensive to fast and expensive, are as follows:

- **Bluetooth**—Not widely available and is not expected to replace the need for high-speed data networks between computers. It was designed to cover only small physical spaces, such as individual rooms. Bluetooth's best use is probably for wireless keyboards and sending commands from a computer to a printer.

- **Infrared Data Association (IrDA)**—Uses infrared light pulses to send signals, just like the trusty TV remote control. Because all remotes use this standard, a remote from one manufacturer can control a device from another manufacturer. But they have to be in direct line of sight with each other to work. Although an IrDA-based network is capable of transmitting data at speeds up to 4 Mbps, the line-of-sight requirement means an access point is needed in each room. That's a problem.

- **Wi-Fi**—The Wi-Fi Alliance certifies equipment based on 802.11 technology. Wi-Fi gear communicates at a speed of 11 Mbps whenever possible over unlicensed frequencies via devices known as hot spots. If signal strength or interference is disrupting data, the devices drop back to 5.5 Mbps, then 2 Mbps, and finally down to 1 Mbps. Though it might occasionally slow down, this keeps the network stable and reliable.

  Wi-Fi, once a grassroots phenom, is taking the networking world by storm. Public venues, such as coffee houses and restaurants, are offering free access to the Internet via Wi-Fi. Manufacturers are rushing to build Wi-Fi capability into new PCs and digital recording devices. Boeing is building Wi-Fi into airplanes. Telephone companies, including Verizon in Manhattan, are converting their phone booths into hot spots.

Finally, there are interesting hybrid solutions emerging, such as the combination of using home power lines to distribute signals among rooms, and after it is inside a room, using a wireless network to sling signals to various devices.

Guarding the Broadband Gates

One potential drawback to an always-on system like broadband is that it's always on. It's similar to always leaving your front door open. It increases the possibility of someone walking in who perhaps isn't there to borrow a cup of sugar, but instead wants to take things.

The insatiable mindset of the computer hacker to find back doors into computer networks, and wreak various kinds of havoc, has been widely demonstrated. At least a few times per year, big hacks make national headlines. Usually, hacking shows up as a virus, inadvertently downloaded into a PC. The electronic tinkering that follows generally falls into the malicious intent category. Computer viruses gave rise to virus protection software, such as that offered by companies like Norton and McAfee. They work by regularly scanning a PC for known viruses, and checking downloadable files while they're downloading, to make sure they're not infected or infectious.

Broadband service providers generally recommend two mechanisms, right from the start, to increase security for their customers. One involves a PC's operating system. Most contemporary operating systems offer a method for PCs to connect to one another over a local-area network (LAN). Setting up a LAN requires setting a parameter in the operating system, known as file sharing, to On. Yet, doing so, without the further protection of a firewall, leaves those files open to sharing with unintended entities.

Which brings us to the second portion of a basic security system for cable and DSL modems: firewalls. *Firewalls* are hardware devices or software packages that protect PCs from unauthorized intrusion, at least up until the point when signals are unleashed into a home network. They do so by blocking and filtering certain incoming packets, based on certain parameters. Maybe the intent is to block a specific IP address, or web domain name, from making any requests for files. Or maybe the intent is to block undesired material by sniffing for packets containing keywords.

Firewalls also come embedded into some equipment, such as cable and DSL routers for home networks. In the case of cable modems, privacy and security mechanisms were built into the original and ongoing versions of the DOCSIS specification. For example, the link between each cable modem and the headend CMTS is generally encrypted, using a technique called *baseline privacy interface*, or BPI. The intent is to provide data privacy across the RF portion of the broadband passageway, by encrypting the traffic flowing between cable modem and CMTS.

The details of how BPI works is beyond the scope of an introductory broadband discussion, such as this book. Essentially, it works, most cable operators use it, and stronger mechanisms of various flavors are in the works and being deployed, as of this writing.

That is not to say that cable modems are completely secure from computer hackers. Nothing is completely secure from computer hackers. A break-in is more a matter of when than if. The best defense, in the case of broadband privacy, is a good offense. Combining commercially available firewall and virus protection software with encryption over the controllable links in a cable modem system are a proactive start. More advanced techniques are well under way. Security, in the end, is a matter of economics: The more you want, the more it costs. Like insurance, it's important to match up your security investment with the value of the data that underlie it—and no more.

Summary

Broadband networks take established data networking principles and apply them over an emerging set of access networks that deliver high capacity rates to the home. Cable television, DSL, and wireless networks are the relatively new solutions to the once-vexing problem of adequate bandwidth beyond the backbone network. Now, with these platforms in place and performing well to deliver broadband connectivity, a final segment of the broadband network is emerging: home networks that allow users to sling fast-moving content such as data, voice, and video to appliances and devices throughout the household. With these advancements come new fears of data intrusion, thanks to broadband's always-on capability, making security systems recommended parts of any residential broadband installation.

CHAPTER 4

WHO GETS BROADBAND?

IF YOU DON'T HAVE A broadband connection to your home, chances are you know someone who does. As of mid 2003, about 19 percent of U.S. households (or around 20 million U.S. homes) had some type of broadband network connection, and there were an estimated 45 to 50 million broadband subscribers worldwide. The deployment of broadband has only begun, and although the patterns are anything but uniform, the unmistakable impression is that broadband is rapidly achieving substantial presence.

Impression is an apt word, given that the business of measuring broadband's progression is based in part on a benefit-of-the-doubt approach to wading through a sea of analysis and data, some of which is rock-solid and some of which represents merely educated guesswork. In the U.S., where the main broadband providers are publicly held corporations that report their progress in rich detail and under the guiding presence of truth-in-reporting laws, divining the total number of broadband-connected households is fairly routine. To wit, Table 4-1 provides an encapsulation of how the vast majority of all U.S. broadband connections were divided up, by provider, in mid 2003. (The final column indicates the number of total connections added during one three-month period, the third quarter of 2002.)

Table 4-4 *Top U.S. Broadband Providers, 2Q 2003*

Provider	Technology	Total Broadband Subscribers	Additions in Latest Three Months
Comcast	Cable Modem	4,388,000	350,900
Time Warner Cable	Cable Modem	2,900,000	170,000
SBC Communications	DSL	2,800,000	304,000
Verizon	DSL	1,900,000	101,000
Cox Communications	Cable Modem	1,700,000	112,452
Charter Communications	Cable Modem	1,349,000	76,700

continues

Table 4-4   *Top U.S. Broadband Providers, 2Q 2003 (Continued)*

Provider	Technology	Total Broadband Subscribers	Additions in Latest Three Months
Cablevision*	Cable Modem	852,835	82,710
Adelphia Communications	Cable Modem	700,000 (est.)	N/A
Qwest Communications	DSL	600,000	65,000
Covad	DSL	453,000**	36,000
Mediacom*	Cable Modem	214,000	24,000
Insight Communications	Cable Modem	179,500	11,200
RCN	Cable Modem	155,809	12,280
CableOne	Cable Modem	106,600	10,800
Total		19,498,744	1,460,042

* 1st Quarter, 2003
* Includes 189,000 Business Connections
Source: Analysis of Company Reports

The numbers, no doubt, will be steadily more impressive with each month that passes. Various researchers note, for example, that broadband will probably pass the 25 percent penetration mark in the U.S. faster than either PCs or mobile telephones did. If you consider the energizing and widespread impacts that these earlier technologies produced, you can begin to sense the potential for broadband. With each new home that is connected to the high-speed, always-on broadband network, more possibility occurs. Already, some businesses have begun to tailor what they do to mesh with the growing broadband community. Many entertainment-oriented websites are fashioning content strictly with a broadband audience in mind, and companies engaged in the still-emerging market for Internet-enabled telephone calls are timing their progression to the steady broadband march.

In other global markets, the handiwork of financial analysis firms and market research companies is leaned upon heavily as the ongoing barometer of broadband's ascension. Either way, a brief scan of the broadband headlines allows no escape from the conclusion that things are moving swiftly in broadband-land:

- The Chilean telecommunications regulator, Subtel, reports that the number of broadband connections in the Latin American country rose by 40 percent during the second quarter of 2002, to 115,660.

- In Latin America at large, a market-analysis firm, The Yankee Group, estimates there will be 1.2 million broadband residential subscribers by the end of 2003, with Mexico leading the growth charge, nearly tripling its anticipated number of DSL customers.

- The technology research firm Forrester Research projects the number of broadband households in Western Europe will rise to 38 million by 2006.

- Nearly a third of all online/Internet households in Japan are now connected to a broadband network, reports Japan's Ministry of Public Management. In December of 2002 alone, the number of Japanese DSL households rose by more than 500,000, to 5.64 million.

- DSL connections in Australia more than doubled (rising by 112 percent) from March to September 2002, according to the Australian Bureau of Statistics.

- In the third quarter of 2002, U.S. cable television companies added 1.1 million new broadband subscribers—equating to more than 12,000 per day— according to the Leichtman Research Group.

- Between November 2001 and November 2002, broadband subscriptions in the U.K. nearly tripled, rising 272 percent.

- Point-Topic estimates the total worldwide number of DSL households nearly doubled in 2002, from 18.8 million to 36.3 million.

- New broadband subscriptions in the U.S. increased by 400 percent between June 2000 and June 2002, according to the Pew Internet & American Life Project.

- Even more impressive than the number of households connected to broadband networks will be the number of different devices connected to broadband networks. Forrester analysts project there will be 191 million devices connected to broadband networks by 2005.

In sum, broadband is growing fast. More than 100 million people now have access to residential broadband networks worldwide, and as noted previously, roughly 45 million households now subscribe to a broadband service. The Americas represents about half of all broadband residential subscribers, with the Asia-Pacific region comprising 37 percent, and Europe, about 16 percent.

In the U.S., of the total number of broadband households, about two-thirds receive broadband network connections from the local cable TV company, most of the remainder subscribe to a broadband service from the local phone company, and a relatively small number get broadband from satellites or new wireless networks. Worldwide, the pattern is reversed, with telephone-based DSL networks the most prominent means of broadband delivery. It's worth noting that the numbers themselves are only fleeting snapshots. Undoubtedly, by the time you read this there will have been substantial increases; the point is that broadband is growing rapidly throughout most of the developed world.

One of the reasons it's worth capturing this momentum on paper is that in broadband's march to prominence, a potentially profound transition in worldwide community exists. Broadband has the capability to deliver on the Internet's (and arguably Marshall McLuhan's) longstanding promise of the global village. Unlike any communications medium before it—printed books, television, radio, sound recordings—broadband poses uniquely difficult challenges for industrial or government control. The use of television and radio signals, of course, can be regulated with relative ease by governments that control the availability of assigned frequencies necessary to convey them. Books and recordings, physical assets that they are, are subject to distribution controls by those who fear an open discourse or have other reasons for limiting the breadth of ideas to which readers are exposed. Broadband doesn't magically seep into closed societies, of course. It requires networks and expensive technology and the capital to support both, and governments intent on denying it entry can be successful.

What is unique about broadband is its own willingness to accept and distribute ideas and knowledge within the common framework of the network itself. Broadband is unique in that most people connected to broadband networks are effectively connected to everyone else through high-speed, always-on links, and virtually all of them speak a common underlying technical language, that of Internet Protocol (IP).

That's not to imply that broadband networks alone can fix the world's most tragic problems. The unfortunate fact is that the vast majority of people across our planet not only lack access to broadband networks but to modern information technology in general. Still, the fact is that broadband is the stuff of nightmares to those who would close off societies to the rest of the world. After it is deployed, it pulsates with a unique and historically unprecedented mix of ideas, knowledge, and expression available in an instant to any user, anywhere.

This has long been true of the Internet at large, of course, and its global influence cannot be overstated. The media measurement company Nielsen//NetRatings believes that more than half a billion people have access to the Internet. Most users connect from home, although the proliferation of public-access locations, such as Internet cafes, is an important contributor. (In the Arab world, the research firm Madar reports the penetration of the Internet, at 9.23 percent, has now outstripped PC penetration, at 7.64 percent. One reason is the growth of Internet cafes, which numbered more than 9,081 throughout Arab nations as of late 2002.)

Broadband, newer than dialup Internet access and not quite as universally available, still represents a small subset of the total residential Internet landscape. Broadband today represents a minority of all residential Internet connections, ranging anywhere from less than 10 percent to 30 percent in most wired nations. Only in South Korea are the majority of Internet-connected households tied to broadband networks. Yet the gap continues to shrink globally as dialup Internet users exchange slower connections for broadband, and as newcomers to the Internet use broadband as their first means of connecting.

The difference between generic Internet access and broadband, though, is that the amount, breadth, and diversity of content that can be shuttled through a broadband pipe is more impressive than via traditional dialup, slow-moving Internet connections. Equally profound is the persistence, or the always-on nature, of broadband. It's as if a constant communications channel is without fail at the ready throughout the fast-growing worldwide community that is broadband. Finally, as research described elsewhere has shown, broadband simply inspires people to use the Internet in different ways and more often. The possibilities beginning to percolate as a result of this shared global medium are captivating.

Cataloguing snapshots of the broadband user base—45 million residential subscribers or so through the end of 2002—is interesting only up to a point. If that were as good as it gets, we'd hardly be motivated to write, or read, a book about the subject. However, signs are afoot that broadband is only beginning a run to prominence that could rival the growth curves of pervasive media and communication staples ranging from the telephone to the video recorder to the wireless mobile telephone—all elements that have inarguably changed daily patterns of life and community throughout the world.

Overall, broadband has tended to grow fastest in countries where there is either a concerted effort supported by government policy to build out networks, or a relatively permissive regulatory approach that encourages private investment. The large majority of residential broadband users today come from five countries: the U.S., Canada, South Korea, Germany, and Japan.

Typically, these broadband connections are built and promoted as a means to render faster, more satisfying access to the Internet. Payment schemes and pricing vary, but it's not uncommon in the U.S. and elsewhere for residential customers to pay fees of approximately $30 to $50 per month for access to a high-speed Internet connection. Thus, the business of residential broadband, which barely existed five years ago, now generates billions of dollars each month, and is growing still at a double-digit clip each year.

The types of connections making their way into the everyday lives of people across the globe are early examples of what's to come. True broadband can render more than just speedier access to the Internet. It can deliver television signals, telephone calls, and other digital content. Yet for millions of users, even these first-generation broadband networks represent liberation from tedious, slow-moving digital network connections of old. Customers love them.

Faster, Faster

Despite broadband's healthy climb—45 million paying customers in the space of five years—more than a few policy analysts, government researchers, and social theorists worry that the pace of adoption simply isn't fast enough yet to produce meaningful improvements in the way we solve longstanding problems of education, economics, and the environment.

Nor, some believe, has broadband technology yet evolved to the point where we truly have achieved some semblance of the original "information highway" notion— the embodiment of access to any content, anywhere, anytime.

Both points have some foundation. Yes, broadband has a global foothold. Yes, it's growing fast—faster than the telephone and automobile did following their commercial introductions—and yes, millions of citizens have at their disposal broadband networks capable of shuttling enormous amounts of digital data at higher speeds than we've ever encountered before. Still, the medium's tipping point hasn't yet come about. Unlike the Internet, or even the VCR, which have both found their way into a majority of U.S. households, broadband as of today still remains a smallish medium, used by a minority of Internet households as a means of connecting to digital content and communications.

Policy makers and broadband proponents see so much promise in broadband that many would like to see faster deployment and adoption occur. TechNet, a coalition of information technology companies that champions the broadband cause, calls the benefits of broadband on the quality of life "immeasurable," and has challenged the U.S. government to set a goal of making an affordable, 100-Mbps connection available to virtually all U.S. homes by 2010. Similarly, in a September 2002 report on demand for broadband, the U.S. Commerce Department's Office of Technology Policy said that when it comes to a world-class information infrastructure, "there may be no element more critical today than ubiquitous and affordable high-speed Internet—broadband."

Aiming to sway voters in the late 1920s, Herbert Hoover promised a continuation of America's growing prosperity with the signature line: "A chicken in every pot and a car in every garage. Based on the sudden wellspring of broadband-is-good sentiment that has arisen lately, the campaign slogan could be reborn today as a "10-Mbps connection to every home."

From all corners of the global information economy, champions of broadband connectivity have emerged. The role of broadband in advancing our economy is now widely acknowledged. In the USA, a group of top executives from leading technology companies is lobbying the U.S. government to adopt and support goals for widespread broadband availability. "Broadband should be a national imperative for this country in the 21st century, just like putting a man on the moon was an imperative in the last century," says John Chambers, the president and chief executive officer of Cisco Systems and a cofounder of the TechNet broadband advocacy group. "In order to stay competitive, educate the workforce, and increase productivity, the United States must have ubiquitous broadband."

Coalitions of both industry and government are pressing to realize extremely aggressive deployment rates for broadband, literally across the world. Japan's Ministry of Public Management, Home Affairs, Posts and Telecommunications, wants to have an always-on broadband connection available to 30 million homes or more by 2005. The U.S. Federal Communications Commission has established an effort to track broadband availability across the country, aiming to keep tabs on what the FCC's chairman, Michael Powell, calls "the central communications policy objective in America." There have been a handful of bills introduced into the U.S. Congress to spur faster broadband deployment. In Canada, the quest for ubiquitous broadband availability has become a matter of national pride. Canada's National Broadband Task Force calls its goal of networking the nation for broadband "The New National Dream."

Eric Benhamou, the chief executive officer of Palm Computing, the maker of portable information and computing devices, embodies much of the current fervor for broadband availability. He advocates a joint effort by private industry and government to deliver high-speed broadband service into 100 million U.S. homes—nearly the entire country—by 2010. "It has to come from the highest levels," Benhamou says. "From the president, the Congress, the FCC, and on down."

In the U.K., Prime Minister Tony Blair says broadband has the potential to "revolutionize many aspects of our lives. It has the potential to increase productivity, enhance competitiveness and enable new markets to be reached. It could radically improve public services. And it can help rural and remote economies—geographical location will no longer be a restriction to competing with urban rivals."

The president? The British prime minister? Congress? National initiatives to ensure deployment of a new communications service? What's going on here? How did we arrive at the point where an idea to pipe data down a faster communications network became a matter of national priority?

Just as governments recognized in the 1930s that the emergence of highways and road systems were vital to the future, the fact is that broadband is important to economic growth and quality of life, and leaders of both industry and government are recognizing it.

The analogy to national highways is irresistible, if overdone, and the sudden interest in this creation called broadband reflects an understanding that networks support every modern society. Nations with well-constructed, well-maintained networks tend to flourish. Transportation networks carry goods to people, allow people freedom to conduct business in distant places, and allow flexible and convenient travel. Energy networks deliver power and fuel. And communications networks carry information, ideas, knowledge, creativity, and intelligence for organizations and individuals to use. The broadband overlay on our modern communications networks will unleash even more power to continue diminishing the obstacles of time and physical distance.

In the case of broadband, we've already built many of the high-speed throughways—hundreds of thousands of miles of fiber-optic cable backbones that can transport tremendous amounts of information—video, data, pictures, sounds, whatever you want to throw its way—with stupendous speed. Yet ironically, after an over-ambitious effort to plant too much optical fiber into the ground, much of the capacity available from backbone networks remains unused. By some estimates, 90 percent of the backbone data capacity in the U.S. is fallow, and a few of the high-flying companies that built vast fiber networks have collapsed under the pressure of less-than-expected demand, and, in some highly publicized incidences, questionable accounting practices that overstated demand. As a result, the market has failed to materialize as projected. Fiber lines literally are laying in wait for something to do because of the relatively small percentage of homes and businesses actually connected to these hearty backbone lines. It has been far easier to build the initial backbone of broadband than it has been to complete the loop—the so-called "last mile" that connects homes and businesses to this capacity.

Even so, thanks to a rising demand by consumers, plus healthy competition between cable and telephone providers, private industry has arisen to fill in the remaining gap—the last mile—of the high-speed network chain. The good news for those who see broadband as a key economic driver is the fact that the residential broadband market has grown impressively even as economic conditions in the telecommunications and dot.com sectors were blighted.

Broadband is important both as an economic force and a quality-of-life force. The U.S. Commerce Department reports that the surging use of information technology in general (including computer hardware, software, and communications equipment) was responsible for two-thirds of the acceleration in total economic productivity growth in the second half of the 1990s. Yet, we've connected only a small fraction of the world's households to broadband networks that can distribute the products of the information-technology to a wider populace.

Broadband promises big things not just for economic productivity, but for the character of our societies. The Internet itself is a vast technological leap on an age-old theme associated with names like Gutenberg and Carnegie—that the distribution of knowledge lifts our collective societies, educates and empowers individuals, and contributes to our social and economic vitality.

The Internet's promise of access to information, entire libraries of research and, literally, a world of knowledge has no doubt empowered millions to improve their lot in life. Before the mid-1990s, when the development of the World Wide Web and affordable (or free) browsers made the Internet available to the general public, much of the knowledge stored within computer networks remained accessible only to a relatively few people. (The rest went to the library to do research.) Today, the Internet and its vast amount of content is available to just about anyone with a telephone connection to their home.

Yet with all the enthusiasm behind broadband, and a broad coalition of industry and government powers seemingly in favor of rapid deployment, students of the emerging broadband network medium might be moved to ask why broadband isn't moving along even faster. After all, the consumer math seems to lie squarely in the broadband camp. Consider that a typical residential Internet service provider (ISP) charges roughly $25 a month to provide a household with access to the Internet, e-mail, and associated benefits. The cost for a separate telephone line that sustains Internet connectivity while freeing up the primary line for phone calls runs $15 to $20. The combination of those two costs, around $40 to $45 a month, is roughly equal to what consumers pay a typical cable modem or DSL provider for both pieces of the puzzle: network access and a dedicated line to provide it. Of course, the experience is also inarguably better over broadband. Data flow much faster and the connection is always on. Why then, haven't millions more users made the seemingly easy conversion to broadband?

One reason might be inertia. Individuals and families within Internet-connected households might be perfectly content to scan e-mail messages and browse websites with the support of their trusty incumbent ISP. Well-documented evidence also suggests that many dialup customers stay with dialup purely out of concerns over having to change their e-mail addresses should they sign up with a new broadband provider.

Dialup customers might have other reasons to be reluctant to take the broadband plunge. True, data rates in excess of 1 Mbps deliver a more responsive Internet experience. However, video files and large graphics files can still take longer than preferred to download, and streaming media—on-demand video clips, music, and more—can fail to live up to the experience available in the family room, where the trusty television set awaits.

Too, the security of communications associated with broadband is a concern for a growing number of would-be users. The always-on connectivity that is a hallmark of broadband's allure and ease-of-use also opens the door for abuse. Most broadband providers today offer or recommend the installation of firewall security resources designed to prevent unscrupulous intruders from using the persistent connectivity of broadband to snoop into the innards of connected devices.

A final thread of thought is that broadband simply hasn't yet come up with the right combinations of discounted pricing and enhanced applications to truly sway the masses.

Inevitably, those twin dynamics will emerge, to the benefit of consumers. Already, the broadband marketplace has racked up enough users to inspire numerous content providers to load up their services with engaging, appealing content. Moreover, competition already is driving higher data rates and lower retail prices.

Broadband Drivers Wanted

Major League Baseball games now are available, for example, not just over television but over the Internet—provided a user has a suitably swift broadband connection and is willing to pay a modest subscription fee. There are video streams and audio files aplenty that play nicely over broadband and poorly over dialup. Hollywood, too, is getting into the game with new on-demand broadband movie services that let users summon the latest hits directly over a broadband Internet connection.

These emerging content vehicles, noteworthy as they might be, are examples of only one narrow application—residential entertainment—that is likely to help drive the next phase of broadband adoption. Briefly, here are capsules of additional applications and features that, coupled with increasingly attractive retail subscription fees, are apt to tilt the Internet-connectivity balance in favor of broadband.

Business Applications

One of the greater laments for the last five years has been the dearth of broadband Internet connections outside of the workplace. It started when professionals became accustomed to local-area networks that transfer files to other PCs and printers at blink-of-an-eye speeds. It continued through fast Internet connections. It's not over yet.

New communications advances typically are introduced first to businesses — chiefly because of affordability issues — and later to residential users. The axiom is certainly true of broadband's first emphasis: Internet connections. These days, and for the foreseeable future, broadband isn't only known and appreciated in the workplace; it is expected.

Still, today's broadband should only be thought of as Broadband 1.0. High-speed access to the Internet is great, and it's worthy of the broadband prefix, but only as a starting point. As more and more services become available based on the underlying mechanisms of the Internet and IP, more and more businesses will rely on broadband to streamline operational costs.

Some examples of cost savings are obvious: With videoconferencing systems that are connected at each end by a managed, broadband link — so the experience isn't more annoying than productive — there's a positive impact on travel costs. That's just one example. The University of California-Berkeley's 2002 study, Net Impact, gauged the cost savings of Internet and e-business initiatives on U.S. organizations at $155 billion through 2001. Thanks to the impact of high-speed connectivity, the study suggests those cost savings could swell to $500 billion by 2010.

Part of broadband's contribution to business and industry is making affordable access to communications power available to small and independent businesses. Such access was once available only to billion-dollar corporations. Large companies have had access to data networks and storage technology since the 1970s — but at large-company prices. The advent of the Internet, followed by the availability of inexpensive broadband connections, has empowered businesspeople to accomplish more and produce more, often with fewer underlying resources.

Broadband also offers a direct conduit for businesses to do business. In March 2000, the U.S. Bureau of the Census found that during the fourth quarter of 1999, online sales by retail establishments totaled $5.3 billion, or 0.64 percent of all retail sales, and more recent private-market estimates suggest big increases have occurred since. Those businesses that sell goods online await a bigger presence for broadband, because the broadband channel enables so many more ways to present and promote merchandise and services.

There is a much larger market for using data networks to conduct business between companies. Estimates suggest hundreds of billions of dollars of business is now transacted over broadband Internet networks, as organizations buy goods, manage inventories, streamline purchasing processes, and otherwise integrate broadband into their daily processes.

Government Applications

For government, broadband networks can hasten what the Internet started: a progression from standards of centralization to standards of distribution.

Online access to the democratic process already is allowing citizens to be more aware of, and participate more fully in, representative government. Citizens can receive updates on legislation via online networks, e-mail representatives with views and suggestions, and engage in the political process with more ease than ever. As in all areas of life, the Internet eliminates or bypasses barriers, including those blocking citizens from lawmakers and government-led initiatives. The entryways to government are no longer the physical doors and gates of imposing buildings, but digital portals available at a click online.

Broadband, once again, poses a way to further the online advance of government and citizen's access to it. Thanks to C-SPAN, a cable television public affairs network, it has been possible for years for viewers to watch the U.S. Congress at work. Yet until the onset of broadband, the relative scarcity of distributed bandwidth made it impossible for citizens to have similar access to other bodies of government. With broadband, it becomes possible to observe live sessions not only of federal legislative bodies, but state governments, city councils, even the workings of the municipal court system.

Broadband affords governments the opportunity to communicate in a richer fashion than merely posting forms and text documents on websites. Law enforcement agencies can more readily seek the involvement of citizens in keeping watch for lawbreakers. Common tools of law enforcement rarely available to the public — videotaped evidence, audio alerts, and more — can ride along the broadband network. Rather than intrude on constitutional protections, broadband can reinforce them, by inviting a broader segment of the public to literally look in on the daily workings of elected officials and government institutions.

Governments also are making use of high-speed broadband connections to make the daily process of government more efficient and convenient. In Texas, nearly a third of vehicle owners in Harris County now renew their vehicle registrations online. In Virginia, the Department of Transportation has rolled out broadband connections to rest-station kiosks that allow travelers to get current weather and traffic information from the road — and even book a hotel room in the next city if they want.

The most profound impact of broadband communications on government, though, is likely to be a furthering of democratic principles throughout the world. Governments that insist on tyrannical imposition thrive when access to information is limited. Over time, broadband connectivity reduces the ability of any single institution to control access to information and to enforce artificial standards of behavior. Let's not be naïve. Broadband still seems a distant dream in a world where millions of people can't even make a telephone call. However, broadband does have the power to make available more information, more diversity of thought, and more freedom of expression—all enemies of tyranny.

Health-Care Applications

Walk into any doctor's office and you'll be overwhelmed with analog. There's paper everywhere. Shelves upon shelves of manila-colored patient file folders dominate the office landscape, as if to boast the size of the doctor's practice. You're told to sign-in upon arrival. You fill out a multipage medical history and turn that in with your medical insurance card. Before you leave the office, the receptionist flips through a paper calendar in an attempt to book your next appointment in the near future.

If tests are needed, you have to fill out more paperwork. Patients who have had to undergo magnetic resonance imaging or X-rays are often required to shuttle their films from one doctor's office to another.

A broadband network potentially enables the elimination of all that clutter and disorganization. A patient might input his or her medical history into a small electronic pad once, and then share it with other doctors, when necessary. Patient files would be digitized and stored. Using that raw data, doctors could spot local trends about illnesses, identify common symptoms, and attend proactively to new outbreaks.

Medical office receptionists could schedule upcoming appointments more efficiently, or even let the patient do that unassisted via a broadband enabled, touch-screen computer, much like those used by airlines today to allow travelers to check in and select their seat without going to the check-in counter.

Moving beyond the office environment, the further benefit of a broadband network is its ability to allow medical experts to collaborate, share information, and view X-ray films—all without leaving their offices.

Patients with chronic illnesses—such as diabetes, asthma, and heart disease—could wear small detection devices on their bodies that would monitor their health on a minute-by-minute basis. Unacceptable changes in blood chemistry or heart rate could be instantly analyzed. If a real health risk is detected, the patient's doctor could be informed. Even today, patients with rare diseases get together online in virtual help-groups to educate themselves and others about their conditions and options for treatment.

Similar detectors could be used to monitor public locations that could be targets for terrorism, such as subways, train stations, and other places where the public gathers. Air-quality detectors could be tied to a broadband network that would provide a way to warn the public of a problem and seek help from police, fire, and medical personnel.

Using broadband to collapse response times to both public and private emergencies can help save lives and lower the cost of insurance by transitioning the medical industry from reactive to proactive. Imagine the cost savings (to say nothing of the life saving) that would be realized if a heart patient could be treated before he collapsed and had to be rushed to the emergency room.

Educational Applications

If the key to education is personalizing the information mix for each student, there's tremendous value in broadband. For starters, just about everything remote becomes local: The elementary student in Des Moines who is researching stalactites and stalagmites, can take a virtual field trip to Wales to get a nearly first-hand look. Flipping through old issues of *National Geographic* (which, despite broadband, is always fun) can be augmented by live conversations with the children of a tribal village in South Africa.

There are practically as many examples of how broadband localizes remote places as there are remote places to localize.

Learning becomes more participative with broadband. Traditional lecturing methods give way to collaboration among students, teachers, and peers—even across scholastic boundaries. Access to teachers widens. With next-generation broadband, students might be able to pick their teachers. The classroom itself becomes less dependent on physicality. A classroom is anywhere a lesson is received.

Most cable and telephone companies offer broadband Internet services to public schools for free. Universities, both public and private, are more often than not wired for broadband in every dorm room. With the infrastructure in place, it's not at all inconceivable to anticipate a future broadband learning environment that moves the content of learning—video clips, database distillations, information—closer and closer to students. The dorm room becomes the library.

Federal regulators are well aware of broadband's potential impact on schools. In February 2002, U.S. Representative John Larson introduced legislation to create a $30 million National Science Foundation program aimed at pushing broadband further into public schools. "The point of the bill," Larson said, "is to create a skilled, trained pipeline of students...to develop the kind of workforce that America needs in the future."

Today's students—and users of current broadband networks—will be the true pullers and pushers of next-generation broadband networks. What seems useful and new to today's adult broadband users seems everyday and to-be-improved-upon by today's third-graders.

Entertainment Applications

With broadband as its companion, entertainment might become a more personalized experience, where consumers are empowered to watch, listen to, or interact with the programs, music, and content they choose, at a time that's convenient for them.

Whether downloaded or streamed live, digital video files are large. They need broadband in the same way tall ships need drawbridges—just to get through. Because of the bandwidth and delivery demands of large video and music files, broadband is the medium for which entertainment has long been waiting. Complicated copyright issues and rights-management questions still must be solved, but without question, broadband networks will allow people to have a more direct say in what they see, hear, and enjoy.

On the flipside, broadband offers more producers of content more avenues through which they can reach potential fans. The Long Beach, California rock band, Sublime, developed a loyal fan following in its early years purely by virtue of Internet exposure. This story is likely to be repeated as creative people have a chance to develop direct relationships with audiences without the interference and control of studios, record labels, and assorted middlemen.

Consumers will be able to select from literally hundreds of entertainment and educational choices, a list that could include the previous day's sporting events or the latest episode of their favorite drama. Sports aficionados who want to see the 1993 Super Bowl again can do so. Fans of ABC's *20/20* news program can view a segment they missed a week, or a year, earlier.

A vast amount of content will be compiled, categorized, and stored in local servers and made available over broadband connections to a variety of display devices. Consumers will navigate through lists of content and be able to search using key words, genres, titles, actor names, and other filters.

In addition to vastly increasing the variety of programs available to consumers, broadband will also improve the image/audio quality of what's consumed. By converting virtually everything to digital technology, television and movies will look and sound better than ever before.

As the film industry transitions to an all-digital environment, consumers will also be able to enjoy perfect copies of the latest box-office hit. Those annoying scratches and audio "pops" that spoil an otherwise excellent product by creating distractions will be eliminated. Movie theaters will more easily be able to show the latest hit on multiple screens because all screens will have simultaneous access to the same movies. Hollywood studios can save millions of dollars in duplication and distribution costs by switching to digital media. Instead of having multiple copies of a major film make its way to the black market, studios can protect their assets via encrypted delivery over a broadband distribution network.

The advertising systems that now subsidize billions of dollars in entertainment content and distribution will follow some of the same general trend lines as entertainment itself. Advertising will become—and already is becoming—more personal and relevant to the entertainment consumer, by employing intelligence about characteristics volunteered by the viewer.

Although I'd hardly call my home movie of our family's New Year's festivities "entertainment" for anyone that's not in our family, the movie was nevertheless created on a digital camera. Already, computer software exists for everyday people, with their everyday digital cameras, to add fades, musical effects, and all the tools traditionally used by filmmakers in video editing suites. Only one thing is missing: a way to shuttle it, electronically and quickly, to other family members who live far away. Broadband will suit that role just fine.

Summary

In summary, broadband is encroaching rapidly into human affairs and daily life across the globe. With 45 million residential subscribers and counting, broadband is infiltrating households at a faster rate than PCs and mobile telephones did in the U.S. True, slower dialup connections still dominate the market for residential Internet access, but the gap is narrowing as users ditch their dialup modems for high-speed cable, DSL, and wireless connections. Credit goes primarily to private industry for solving the last-mile gap that historically has prevented residential users from enjoying higher-speed access to data networks. Although the broadband adoption pace is impressive, it's possible that an ever greater momentum will occur as competition drives retail connection prices down, and as a flurry of compelling new applications arrives to convince more residents that broadband—like the PC, the television, and the telephone before it—is a requisite of modern life.

CHAPTER 5

THE BROADBAND HOME

NOW, A COUPLE OF words about those broadband people: They're busy.

Like the widespread availability of electrical power did to communities in the early 1900s, the infiltration of broadband into the home is starting to change the way people live and behave. Electricity gave us home washing machines, refrigeration, and the ability to sustain light long into the night. Broadband provides millions of residential users with the tools to learn, work, interact, and communicate in new ways.

Kevin Brinks is one of these residential users. A work-at-home sales representative who sells high-technology image scanners, Brinks is a member of the broadband revolution. Armed with a high-speed DSL connection that's fed through a home network to four PCs within his house, he routinely transmits large data files to clients from his basement office in a matter of seconds. "With dialup, that was taking me 25 minutes each time," Brinks says.

What's equally notable is the influence of the broadband "always-on" connection on his family. From a downstairs bedroom, Brinks' teenage son plays video games on the Internet with opponents who live miles—or even continents—away. His wife, Kati, has become accustomed to checking a PC perched in the living room several times a day to read e-mails and surf the Internet for everyday information (such as weather reports, movie listings, and more). "Any time she wants to research anything—local information or whatever—she just pops on there, types a couple of keywords, and moves on," says Brinks.

Although they might not realize it, the Brinks family of suburban Denver is part of a revolution changing the way people work, learn, and communicate. Broadband connectivity inspires changes in the way millions of worldwide users conduct their daily affairs.

It's also encouraging them to spend more time roaming the world of interactive media at large. Compared with people who connect to the Internet in the old-fashioned narrowband way, broadband users are online more, and when they are online, they do more. For one thing, broadband users are big consumers of entertainment and information that's streamed over the Internet. A growing bounty of this material is available, ranging from breaking news reports to hundreds of live radio feeds from stations around the world. Studies show that broadband users are far more apt than dialup users to tune in. Also, broadband users are fast becoming notorious for the penchant of downloads—music, software, and more—that can be captured more quickly, thanks to broadband's faster data rates.

A taste for streaming audio and file downloads is just one characteristic that defines the growing broadband community. Another striking finding of one research effort into broadband behaviors is that people who have broadband at home spend nearly as much time on the Internet as they do watching television or listening to the radio (about 21 percent of their total daily "electronic media time"). That's a big departure from households with narrowband Internet access, who typically spend just 11 percent of their electronic media usage on the Internet, according to a 2000 study by the media research firm Arbitron. The survey of 3,283 people, called "The Broadband Revolution: How Superfast Internet Access Changes Media Habits in American Households," found that people in broadband households spent an average of 134 minutes daily on the Internet. That's 61 percent more time than the 83 minutes per day spent by people in dialup households.

Before we draw any breathless conclusions about the broadband user revolution, note that broadband users tend to be younger, better educated, and earn higher incomes than people with dialup. Those factors might have some bearing on the behaviors exhibited by the broadband community. But, let's not quibble too much. Anyone who has been liberated from long file-download times and poor playback of streaming audio or video can readily understand why broadband users would want to partake of these features more frequently. Over broadband, downloads actually work well.

The disparities between broadband users and dialup Internet users are even more dramatic when viewed by age. The most prolific broadband users are 18 to 24 year-olds, who report that they spend three hours a day on the Internet, according to a 2001 follow-up study from Arbitron.

As you'd imagine, the notion that broadband compels people to spend more time on the Internet and relatively less time with television has sent many a television-programming executive into panic mode. Television networks and programmers have scurried to develop business models that might allow them to retain their traditional presence in the daily lives of consumers, whether that happens to occur through television or through broadband. A similar search for presence on the new broadband platform has occurred in the movie and music industries, with no one yet having claimed the perfect business model. (One comforting fact for captains of the television industry, perhaps, is the finding that broadband users tend to be incorrigible multitaskers: Twenty-five percent of the respondents to the Arbitron 2002 study reported that they frequently watch television while using the Internet.)

But driving people from the tube isn't the only thing broadband seems to accomplish. With fast access to Internet content and—importantly—easier ways to contribute their own content to others, broadband users have truly become a unique breed. Compared to "average" Internet users, they tend to do more activities with the

Internet, do them more frequently, and do them for longer periods of time. As Table 5-1 shows, a substantially higher percentage of broadband users engage in virtually every type of online activity when compared to dialup users.

Table 5-1   *An Average Day for Internet Users*

Activity	Broadband Users[*]	Dialup Users[*]
Communications		
E-mail	67%	52%
Instant messaging	21%	14%
Chat rooms	10%	5%
Information seeking		
News	46%	24%
Job-related research	36%	14%
Look for product information	32%	18%
For school or training	24%	9%
Look for travel information	23%	6%
Look for medical information	21%	8%
Information producing		
Share computer files with others	17%	4%
Create content (such as web pages or post to bulletin boards)	16%	3%
Display/develop photos	14%	1%
Store files on Internet	8%	N/A
Download		
Download games, videos, pictures	22%	4%
Download music	17%	6%
Download movies	5%	N/A
Media streaming		
Watch video clips	21%	6%
Listen to music/radio stations	19%	4%
Watch movies	4%	N/A

continues

Table 5-1   *An Average Day for Internet Users (Continued)*

Transactions		
Bank online /pay bills online	22%	6%
Buy a product	21%	3%
Buy a travel service	14%	2%
Participate in auctions	10%	3%
Buy groceries/household goods	6%	1%
Buy/sell stocks	5%	1%
Gamble	2%	N/A
Entertainment activities		
Hobby information	41%	18%
Browse just for fun	39%	21%
Play a game	22%	10%
Visit adult websites	6%	1%

* % of each group who engage in various Internet activities on a typical day online.

Source: Home Broadband Users, Pew Internet & American Life Project. February 2002 Survey.

The Pew Internet & American Life Project, which is based on telephone interviews with 507 adult Internet users in early 2002, represents one of the most penetrating looks into the way broadband users interact with the network. Authors John Horrigan and Lee Rainie identified three primary features of home broadband users:

- **They create and manage their own content**—One of the positively inspiring aspects of broadband is its ability to encourage users not only to consume content, but to create it.

    About 40 percent of broadband users have been creating their own content for publication over the Internet (in the form of personal or family websites and online diaries), according to Pew's study. On an average day, 17 percent of broadband users share data files (photos, documents, and music) with others. In each instance, these behaviors occur more frequently with broadband users than dialup users. "People are not passive recipients of media," noted Rainie, director of the Pew Internet study on broadband users, "They are creators and distributors, too."

Broadband's capability to make it easier to distribute large and small files might be inspiring a rebirth of the Internet's original promise: to provide a peer-to-peer network that enables users to easily share information. With a rising corporate and organizational influence, the Internet has become largely a client/server model, wherein large numbers of users extract data from centralized web servers (think Amazon.com). Broadband won't do away with the client/server model by a long stretch, but it does present a platform that makes it more likely that users will increasingly stamp their individual imprint over the network. The rise of sophisticated classification systems that make it easy to search for and download music recordings from user communities is living proof that broadband and related new applications have facilitated this migration from client/server to peer-to-peer computing.

- **They use their always-on connections to satisfy their queries**—The Pew Internet authors found that the persistent connection offered by broadband enables users to turn to the Internet for all sorts of information needs. Sixty-eight percent of broadband users say that they do more information searching online because of their always-on, high-speed connection.

  About 90 percent of users said the Internet has improved their ability to learn new things, and nearly 50 percent said that the Internet has improved their ability to get health-care information. In each instance, when compared to dialup users, broadband users are more apt to credit the Internet with helping them get information that's relevant to their lives. Lots of broadband users credit the always-on nature of broadband with making it easier to find information. There's something elegant and powerful about the ability to turn to the Internet on a whim, conduct a brief search, and find something out without having to endure the delay of initiating a new dialup session.

- **They do many activities online in a typical day**—The high-speed connection enables broadband users to perform multiple tasks throughout the day.

  Broadband users are online at least once a day, which is more than narrowband users. More than 80 percent of broadband users said they're online on a given day; only 58 percent of dialup users said the same.

When contrasting broadband users and dialup users, the downloading and file-sharing disparity is particularly acute.

For every one narrowband Internet user who downloads music or swaps files with others, there are approximately three broadband users who snatch music, movies, and other online content, or make files available to others. That's no surprise. At a broadband connection rate of 1 Mbps, downloading a three- or four-minute music "single" can be accomplished in 20 seconds or less. The same song would take four agonizing minutes to capture over a 56-kbps connection. It's as if broadband data rates have expanded the range of media and information we share and exchange—from simple text e-mails to peer-to-peer delivery of voice, video, and more.

The possibilities for even more enthusiastic usage rates for music become easy to contemplate as connection speeds rise over time. A broadband network operating at a super-fast data rate of 64 Mbps could deliver to you the entire contents of a 72-minute music album in about the same amount of time it would take to start your car's engine for a trip to the local record store—about five seconds. (Today, while music is feasible, downloaded movies are another story. Even with broadband connections of 1 Mbps, movies and long-form video can require hours to download, and remain more of a novelty than anything else.)

Broadband introduces a similar upswing in the use of so-called streaming content, which is material that comes across the network in real-time, just as a live television or radio broadcast does. Nearly one of every five broadband users in the Pew Internet study say that they routinely listen to streaming music or radio stations over the Internet. Just four percent of narrowband customers say the same.

What's apparent across all major studies of the broadband user is the sheer diversity of activities conducted online. The Pew survey shows that the average broadband user does seven things online daily, such as fetching news reports or sending photos to family members. The average dialup Internet user completes only three tasks on an average day.

But doing more activities online isn't the only attribute of merit for broadband users. Internet users with broadband connections say broadband improves their ability to do many things they're already familiar with in the online world. Table 5-2 shows how broadband users are more apt than slow-connection users to credit the Internet with improving various aspects of their lives.

Table 5-2 *Making Life Better*

How Much, If at All, Has the Internet Improved...	Broadband (Percentage Who Say "A Lot," or "Somewhat")	Dialup (Percentage Who Say "A Lot" or "Somewhat")
Your ability to learn new things	86%	73%
The way you pursue your hobby or other interests	65%	48%
Your ability to do your job	65%	42%
The way you get health-care information	47%	41%
The way you manage your personal finances	42%	25%
Your ability to connect organizations in your local community	31%	23%

Source: Home Broadband Users, Pew Internet & American Life Project. February 2002 Survey.

Those with a big economic stake in the future of the Internet have watched with keen interest the emerging portrait of the broadband user. Executives from America Online (AOL), which operates the single largest connection between the Internet and consumers, observes that, among other things, broadband users tend to grab bits and snippets of content and information from the network throughout the day, a behavior that the company's president, Jonathan Miller, labeled "information snacking" in a 2002 presentation to securities analysts. He's got a point. According to the Pew Internet study, 43 percent of broadband users go online several times a day; only 19 percent of dialup users log on more than once a day. Not only do the number of sessions increase with broadband, but the amount of time spent online and the number of web pages viewed also increases. Sean Kaldor, an executive with the measurement firm Nielsen//NetRatings, studied the behavior of a sample panel of Internet users who had upgraded from narrowband to broadband between December 2000 and May 2001. As Table 5-3 shows, the group's time spent on the Internet rose 70 percent—from a collective 26,000 hours to 44,000 hours.

Table 5-3 *Upgrading to Broadband (Monthly Comparison)*

	Before Upgrade	After Upgrade	Difference (In Percentage)
Time spent online per person (Hours:Minutes)	9:28	12:50	36%
Number of sessions	17.94	25.73	43%
Number of pages	615	1039	69%
Total hours online	26,000	44,000	70%

Source: Nielsen//NetRatings

To be sure, some habits and customs of the broadband household cannot be attributed purely to the availability of broadband. Broadband users in general, or at least the first and earliest adopters, tend to come from homes with higher annual incomes and with larger families than the prevailing norm. Even so, researchers believe that these demographic differences are less important in influencing online behavior than the presence of broadband. "The availability of a broadband connection is the largest single factor that explains the intensity of an online American's Internet use," the Pew study states.

A close look at the broadband user base, and what sorts of activities broadband users do online, supports a recent theory that is popular among analysts of the medium: No single "killer application" drives the use of broadband. In other words, combinations of a multitude of activities, ranging from consuming entertainment to communicating by e-mail or instant messages to buying goods online, are the byproducts of broadband access. Pew's study found that 61 percent of broadband users say they're spending more time online since discarding the old dialup modem and installing a broadband connection. Various applications are responsible for driving this increase in time spent on the Internet:

- Thirty-one percent said the extra time comes from more information searching.
- Nineteen percent said additional e-mailing soaked up their increased Internet time.
- Fourteen percent said they were downloading more movies or music.
- Thirteen percent said online shopping was the reason why they were on the network longer.

There is also a growing sense that broadband users are more apt than dialup users to be willing to spend money on online content. A January 2003 survey of Internet users in Britain, Germany, France, Spain, Italy, and Sweden found that 18 percent of broadband users are willing to pay for video content compared to 11 percent of narrowband users. Broadband users also showed a greater willingness to pay for music and gaming content (reported the survey from Jupitermedia Corp).

Broadband's Liberation from the PC

As the data spin out before us, keep in mind the understanding that a substantial change in online-user behavior is occurring even under the current prevailing constraints on the broadband medium. From its inception to the current time, broadband has been provided almost exclusively as a personal-computer service. Nearly every residential broadband connection today is fed directly to a computer, and whether the application is a movie or an online shopping experience, it's rendered through the lens of a computer monitor.

The emerging broadband models look to the day when the broadband data gets liberated from the confines of the PC and roams freely throughout the household. This vision is encapsulated by the movement to something called the *home network*. It supposes that broadband ultimately finds its way into numerous information and communications appliances, and that broadband becomes not just a PC network, but a home-premises network, wherein a central-receiving device might distribute broadband throughout the home in the way that an electrical junction box distributes electricity to every room.

NOTE	The analogy with electricity only goes so far. Some broadband users have expressed dissatisfaction with the speed and reliability of their connections, which suggests that broadband isn't yet on par with telephone services and electrical power regarding "forget-about-it" reliability.

Already, 69 percent of United States broadband users have multiple computers in the home, according to the Pew Internet study, and more than half of those households have some form of network that connects multiple computers.

More interesting is the notion, albeit further down the road, of allowing broadband to find its way into a broader array of appliances than just home computers, printers, and peripheral devices. A recent television commercial from the appliance maker Whirlpool made the point clear. In it, a homeowner is surprised to find a refrigerator repairman at the doorstep. The refrigerator, linked to a broadband network, placed its own trouble call, prompting the onsite visit. Just idle speculation about a futuristic product? Nope. Magazine publisher *Forbes* reported the European appliance manufacturer Merloni Elettrodomestici of Fabriano has sold more than one million networked appliances (mostly washing machines) that can be controlled through the Internet.

Work is also progressing on the front lines of the much vaunted "convergence" movement, a place where a melding of functionality exists among computer-like devices and entertainment appliances, such as TV sets. For example, Software titan Microsoft and the PC maker Hewlett-Packard have collaborated on a computer called the Media Center PC that can act as a central repository for television and music content that can then be parceled out to networked devices in the home.

The point is, even given the fact that broadband is today imprisoned somewhat through the control of a single device—the PC—users have found a tremendous assortment of things to do with it, and are making meaningful changes in their daily media lives as a result. In fact, after it's in the house, broadband seems highly likely to remain. An April 2001 survey of DSL users by the telephone company SBC Communications found that 63 percent of customers claimed they'd give up their ritual morning coffee before yanking out the DSL line.

The Kitchen PC

The fully rendered home broadband network might not be here yet, but one of the fascinating early byproducts of broadband availability seems to be a redefinition of where the PC fits within the household or within the context of family.

If you own a PC, chances are it's perched comfortably on a desk somewhere in your home. After all, much of what we do over the computer is work. We review e-mail, manage budgets, type letters, and manage schedules. When we're done, we're done. We leave the PC and turn to more interesting and entertaining places in our homes.

The marriage of computers with desks, offices, and places where we typically work testifies to the fact that the PC is mainly associated with jobs and tasks. Even the growing popularity of streaming media and entertainment-oriented websites hasn't done much to move the computer from the office to the living room in most households.

The true information revolution will come when the PC, or some other device that accepts a broadband connection, migrates *en masse* to the most lived-in spaces of the household: the kitchen, den, living room, and bedroom. We spend most of our time in those places. Already, many first-generation broadband families enjoy broadband connectivity in these places, where you'll often find a desktop computer, laptop, a new wireless devices known as a web-pad (think of an electronic Etch-a-Sketch) or a detached laptop screen with touch-screen controls that connects wirelessly to a broadband network.

Having a computer in the kitchen hugely contrasts the typical PC-in-the-office scenario. But, remember that broadband doesn't merely replace a dialup, or narrowband, Internet connection. As we're starting to understand from the anthropology of the broadband household, broadband connections change the way people interact. In some ways, broadband seems to prompt entirely new behaviors and ways of responding to the myriad data streams that now ricochet about the home.

Suddenly, with broadband, PCs can drift from the office or den and mingle in all the right places. This mainstream emergence is more than symbolic. No longer imprisoned in spaces and rooms that are cut off from the remainder of the home, computing devices find new ways to flourish when they're integrated into spaces that are more fundamentally relevant to daily life.

The kitchen, a place where so much daily activity revolves, is particularly prominent in the new world of broadband communications. Outfitted with a broadband connection, a surprising number of users have seen fit to plop their computing devices in the center of the action, at a kitchen desk or makeshift workstation located somewhere between the toaster and the electric can-opener. There, a steady diet of brief encounters and on-the-fly grazing replaces, or at least supplements, the elongated sessions familiar to those of us who have known the Internet as a narrowband creature. For many families, locating the family PC in the kitchen has more to do with safeguarding their children from Internet ne'er do wells, certainly. But nonetheless, a PC in the kitchen, or in a centrally accessible room, is not a PC in a closed-off, remote room used for "work" computing.

Within broadband households, it's common to find users integrating the Internet in their lives in seamless, instinctive ways. We see adults, for example, casually checking over the morning's e-mail while they go about normal tasks to prepare for the day. While the toaster browns the bread, they get an early read on messages from the home office. Teens glance at local weather reports and (hoped-for) news of school closings on snowy winter mornings while searching for their lost pair of socks. In studies contrasting dialup Internet households with broadband households, a pronounced tendency is for the PC to become a more frequently used and widely shared resource.

This is hardly a puzzling phenomenon, of course. Dialup, narrowband users are accustomed to sitting before the computer, attempting to accomplish multiple tasks all in a single session that's bound by two identifiable events: signing on and signing off. There is a defined "start" and an equally apparent "finish" to the typical 40-minute dialup session. Between these two invisible bookends, we attempt to complete our online to-do list.

With broadband, you don't have any sign-on and sign-off periods. The concept of a "session" doesn't exist. The persistent broadband connection means that the network is available whenever you want it. New devices beginning to proliferate in the world of wireless networks illustrate this feature well. They don't need to boot up or go through a four-minute ritual of "coming to life." When you need them, they're there, connected to the network, and ready for you to use. Hand-held devices that gather your e-mail messages are a great example of this concept. They don't boot. They just respond to what you need, instantly.

Again, let's use a television analogy. The programs and channels available on television are, effectively, always available; they swirl invisibly around you as part of the radio frequency of a broadcast or satellite TV network (or tucked within the coaxial wiring of cable television). When you turn your television's "power" button on, images and sounds instantly greet you: The nightly news report. The rock concert. The laugh-track on a syndicated sitcom. The close-up of a flying lizard in a South American jungle. You don't wait for your television to muster a connection. You don't hear the electronic shriek of two modems engaging in a cyber-handshake to establish a dialogue.

In homes with broadband connectivity, you don't wait for the electronic handshake, and no noise signals the initiation of a connection. Silently, the network is ever-present, and so long as your broadband device is turned on, it's available to summon web pages, e-mails, instant messages, and more in the mere fraction of a second that it takes you to press a key or to move a mouse. As one SBC Communications consumer-survey respondent said, "My computer is on 24 hours a day, seven days a week."

Broadband users seem willing to discard the idea that the web is a place full of destinations. Rather, it's a treasure of content that's already here—right now. Again, think of the television model. There's no need to consider television programs as resources that must be fetched from distant places. The fact is that they're right here in the living room, and the mere pressing of a button summons tonight's hockey game obligingly onto the screen. Similarly, broadband users seem to consider their favorite web pages and content providers as resources that are literally already resident in the home, just as common PC applications already reside in the computer.

Here's how one broadband user, interviewed for a study published by the former cable television company MediaOne, described the experience:

> When I first got this service, I couldn't believe this was the Internet. I was in Netscape but it wasn't acting like it usually did.... Now, it just seemed too simple. Switching between (Microsoft) Word and the Internet was like changing channels on the television.

The Anthropology of Always-On

MediaOne, since purchased twice (once by AT&T, and subsequently by Comcast Corp.), was a pioneering provider of broadband, high-speed data services to the home. It began its cable-modem deployments in 1994. In a fascinating study of broadband culture funded by its technology research division, MediaOne Labs, the company conducted what it called an ethnographic investigation of how its broadband customers were using their new service. The idea was to chronicle the changing patterns of online behavior, and, more importantly, how these changes affected the fabric and routine of daily life. MediaOne Labs dispatched researchers (with permission, of course) into the homes of some of the first broadband communications customers in the United States, in eastern Massachusetts, during 1998. There, they observed first-hand, and for the first time, some of the striking differences between narrowband and broadband Internet users, and, by extension, began to glean some of the first ideas about how broadband might change the way people work, play, and interact.

Here are some key findings:

- **Always-on connectivity helped weave the broadband service into the daily lives of broadband users**—By observing users in their homes and studying the tracking logs that showed what web features were used, and when, MediaOne Labs uncovered a striking feature among broadband customers: They seemed to be more casual about the way they used their broadband connections. Study participants might glance for new e-mails as they walked past the PC, chat with a youth sport coach on the phone while simultaneously looking up a weather forecast, or dispatch a quick e-mail message between TV commercials. The constant connectivity of broadband seemed to beckon a level of multitasking absent from narrowband Internet homes. "They bought it for speed," said the MediaOne researchers, "but used it for living."

- **Broadband households used the Internet more**—Not just a modest amount more, but four times as much as the average narrowband, dialup household, according to the report.

  For example, one household studied by MediaOne rang up 17 separate Internet sessions in a single day. The 22.5 hours a week? Simple. Lots of short- and medium-sized bursts of Internet activity added together. Again, the presence of a constant, high-speed data connection invites usage that fits more easily into our busy schedules. The temptation to multitask, or use the Internet at the same time we talk on the phone, pay the bills, or watch the kids, is much more pronounced when we don't have to wait on computers.

- **Prime time is all the time**—Well-established trends exist for residential Internet use by times of day. Narrowband users tend to use the Internet more during the evening, roughly from 6 P.M. to midnight. In part, this pattern reflects a dominant-user arrangement in which one household member, often an adult who works outside the home during the day, is guilty of mono-polizing the Internet connection within the home during the evening.

  Broadband's usage time is different. The heaviest concentration of usage occurs in the morning, although usage is generally dispersed more evenly throughout the day. Typical users tended to integrate the Internet into their morning routine, accounting for the heavy use. Family members checked their e-mail, read news headlines, and scanned weather forecasts. Women that remained home during some or all of the day undoubtedly contributed to the early-riser phenomenon. A telling example: A stay-at-home mom who routinely answered e-mail and scanned sweepstakes entries online while her young child ate breakfast.

- **The PC is the center of attention**—The majority of computers attached to the MediaOne broadband service were placed in so-called "public spaces" within the home—family rooms and kitchens instead of bedrooms and dens. Again, this coming-out is hardly an artifice of savvy marketing. It appears to be a grass-roots dynamic that occurs naturally as more family members, smitten by the ease-of-use and new possibilities allowed by broadband connections, demand equal access to the newly empowered PC. The fact that a device originally conceived as a toy of enthusiasts, then a tool of industrialists, could wind up as a common household appliance is a testament to the tremendous innovation in computing technology, economics, and applications. But, it takes a new sort of force to move the device from the desktop to the countertop. That force is broadband.

What else do we know about broadband users and how they behave over the network? Nielsen//NetRatings, the audience and media measurement company, tells us that even though broadband users represent only a minority of the total Internet-connected households, the people connected to high-speed broadband networks account for the majority of all online time, at least in the United States (and probably globally, too, one suspects). Broadband users spent a cumulative total of 1.19 billion hours online in the month of January 2002, representing 51 percent of the total of 2.3 billion hours spent online. In other words, 21 percent of total online users (the broadband segment) racked up 51 percent of total time online. Without a doubt, broadband seems to be inspiring more use of the digital network.

Here are some more numbers for you: At the time Nielsen//NetRatings made its astounding conclusion about broadband's dominance of total Internet time, an estimated 21.9 million broadband users in the United States had broadband connections at home, and 25.5 million people had broadband access at work. (Of course, many of them are the same people, counted once in each category.) But, it's worth noting that the broadband experience for many people is introduced first in the workplace, where a great number of companies and organizations deliver broadband connectivity to individual computers and devices. Most of us know the common lament of the individual who spends the workday humming across the network at very satisfying speeds and cannot bear to suffer the indignity of a 56-kbps connection at home. Tasting the broadband experience does seem to spoil us all, and after we've seen even a glimmer of the possibilities available through a high-speed data connection, it's difficult to go back to dialup again.

Not surprisingly, there's also good news from broadband for those who hope to sell things over the digital network. Broadband users are more likely than those who connect at narrowband data rates to respond to offers and make e-commerce purchases. In fact, one survey of 1046 broadband network users from early 2002 found that nearly half had spent $500 or more online in the last year, and 63 percent made six or more online purchases in the last year. The survey, commissioned by a Texas company, Broadjump, found that more than one-third of broadband users make at least 11 separate online purchases a year.

Summary

The broadband lifestyle involves new opportunities and capabilities for families whose homes will be outfitted both with services that flow over broadband and with a multitude of devices that interact with these services. Already, we're seeing the effect broadband has on individuals and families, with studies showing broadband users are online more often, and accomplish many more things while online, than dialup Internet users. Education, medical care, energy management, and family interactions are just some of the features of daily life that will be improved by broadband networks in the forthcoming "smart" home. Personalized for each household and able to bring a wealth of global knowledge directly to the home, broadband's impact is enormous. Like electricity before it, broadband will bring an enormous wealth of possibility to individuals and families alike.

CHAPTER 6

PLANET BROADBAND

WE ARE LITERALLY DRIVING ourselves crazy. The typical rush-hour commute in a major U.S. metropolis has become a maddening, frustrating crush of cars, fueled by oil pulled from the earth, and consumed at a mind-boggling rate of 3.5 billion gallons a day. Although the U.S. population grew by 20 percent from 1982 to 1997, the time spent by U.S. motorists navigating traffic climbed 235 percent, according to a report produced by the Texas Transportation Institute, which monitors U.S. traffic congestion. Traffic costs the United States $78 billion annually, representing 4.5 billion hours of wasted time and nearly 7 billion gallons of fuel wasted while drivers sit in traffic. What used to be termed rush hour has in fact doubled in less than 20 years, now accounting for six hours a day in the nation's major cities. Congested travel periods now consume nearly half of the daylight hours in a given workday.

It's easy to see why. Seventy-six percent of workers drove to work alone in 2000, according to the latest data from the U.S. Bureau of the Census. That's up three percent from 1990. Not only do most commuting cars carry only one occupant, people are spending more time driving and traveling longer distances to get to work.

The question is, why? True, if your job requires you to haul physical goods, make on-site service calls, fix garage doors, or deliver pizzas, you have no choice but to join this throng of vehicles along the roads and highways. Yet, most people who work move something other than physical goods. They move information.

You are probably familiar with this common early morning ritual: After dressing and gulping down a quick breakfast, you head out to do battle on the road. Destination: the office building. Forty-five minutes later, you pull into a parking space, shut down the engine (you've probably burned one or two gallons of gasoline by now), enter the building, ride the elevator or climb the stairs to your workspace. Then, what's the first thing you do? Stressed and tired from the clogged roadways, you plunk right down to check your voice mail and read your e-mail. You do it. I do it. Millions of office workers do it every day.

In fact, we actually spend a good portion of the day responding to messages from other people and originating messages of our own. In almost all these instances, we're interacting with the same fundamental ingredient: a digital media stream over a telecommunications network.

The sounds you hear when you listen to that first voice mail message from your telephone handset are reconstituted digital bits, or the 1s and 0s of the computing age. The voice you're listening to was sampled by a recording device that understands how to turn each note, inflection, pause, and pitch into a corresponding slice of digital code. The message, in turn, is stored on your company's voice-message server, which is essentially a dedicated computer. When you listen, you're engaging in what telecommunications engineers call a session, or an interplay across a network that distributes digital bits—the network doesn't care if they happen to represent a phone message or a slide presentation—to someone who requests them.

It's going to be a busy day. You've now gone through the morning's first barrage of voice mails, made notes to call people back, deleted some messages, and saved others.

Now you turn your attention to your desktop computer. Or, if you're one of the inveterate multitaskers of our busy age, you're working your e-mail at the same time you're catching up on your phone messages. Either way, essentially, it's the same sequence, only through a different device. Your e-mail inbox dishes up a cauldron of urgent messages, FYIs, follow-ups, and computer file attachments. They all say something different, yet they're all constituted from the same underlying fabric of 1s and 0s. This digital DNA is the stuff of our modern work lives. It zings across networks and bubbles up to the surface on computer screens, wireless phones, and voice-message systems.

I don't know what your own work rituals are. I do know, from observing my colleagues and my own tendencies, that in a ten-hour workday, I might spend six or seven hours on the phone and in front of my computer, corresponding via e-mail, and managing information. The remaining hours are spent visiting face-to-face with colleagues or engaged in meetings that require physical presence. Or at least they seem to, because right now we have no proven alternative.

So, if you're like me, you've navigated the daunting paths of your city's highways and side streets (for an amount of time that always seems too long) in order to hoist yourself in front of two information appliances—your computer and your telephone set—that were available in your home the entire time you were commuting. The information you spent a good portion of your morning receiving and originating didn't care where you were physically located when you interacted with it. For all it knew, you could have been sipping tea on a hilltop dairy farm in Switzerland. As long as you had access to a network, your bits could have found their way to you.

In a more practical scenario, given that most of us don't have the luxury (or interest) to conduct our work from Swiss dairy farms, it is probably possible for you to do the exact same work you spent the last hour doing right from your home, without ever firing up the 6-cylinder, finely tuned engine under the hood of your car, or waiting impatiently at two dozen stoplights, or finding yourself nearly side-swiped by a hurried commuter in a silver Toyota.

The Telework Revolution

It's worth recounting the preceding scenario, despite how many times you've heard it before, as a reminder that we sometimes continue to engage in traditional behaviors and ways of doing business even when viable alternatives are available. Much of the work that goes on today can be done, rather successfully, without the intrusion of a physical journey from point A to point B. In fact, many people are doing just that.

Estimates tend to vary widely, but even a cursory review of your own personal acquaintances will probably turn up a teleworker or two. Overall, one in five employees in the U.S., or about 28.8 million total employees, participate in some form of teleworking, or doing work at a location that's not specific to the work itself, according to a 2001 study conducted by Old Dominion University's Social Science Research Center in Norfolk, Virginia. That doesn't mean they work full-time from home, but engage at least some of the time in working from a remote location, whether it's home, a satellite office, or on the road. Most of them are satisfied with their telework experience and prefer to continue working away from the office.

Three-fourths of those who telework report significant increases in their productivity and work quality — not a surprising finding to those who have experienced the relative bliss of an interruption-free morning in front of the computer and away from the office.

Globally, telework seems to be on the rise, too, although definitive research is scarce, and even those who attempt to track the world's population of teleworkers admit to a certain amount of guesswork. Part of the problem in tracking telework statistics is that definitions vary. Is a teleworker someone who works full-time from home or someone who occasionally works on projects away from the office? We await the verdict still. In the meantime, there's little agreement yet on precise definitions. Even so, by almost any measure or standard, the idea of telework is rising in incidence and prominence.

The Japan Telework Association estimates the nation's population of teleworkers will rise to 4.4 million by 2005 from 2.6 million in 2000. The European Commission estimates at least 9 million teleworkers among member nations. In Finland, where one of Europe's smallest populations is spread over a large geographic area, close to 7 percent of employees routinely work from home using telecommunications networks.

Overall, about 11 percent of workers worldwide telecommuted at least part of the time in late 2001, according to a survey of 1000 companies by the advertising firm Euro RSCG Worldwide, and half of all employees were interested in telework.

The International Telework Association & Council (ITAC), which sponsored the Old Dominion research, estimates the number of U.S. employees who telework has increased 17 percent in the space of a year. Broadband often gets, and probably deserves, some of the credit for inspiring or enabling more teleworkers.

"Today's remote employees are teleworking in the same way the Wright brothers were flying in 1903," said Bruce Mehlman, the assistant secretary for technology policy in the U.S. Commerce Department, in a September 2002 speech. "Pervasive, high-bandwidth computing will transform work from home or remote locations as thoroughly as it is transforming office-based business processes."

Good for us? Possibly. I'm reminded of a television commercial that aired in the late-1990s, just around the time that broadband Internet services began rolling into towns across the U.S. In it, a young professional waltzed around the house in her robe and slippers while connected via telephone and computer to her home office. The commercial, which promoted a new fiber-optic network from the communications company MCI, displayed the prowess of the fully connected telecommuter. The employee in the commercial casually uploaded a slide presentation in real-time for the benefit of a group of crisply dressed colleagues who were huddled around a conference table in a presumably distant place, which I imagined to be New York City. The commercial ended with a line that spoke to the protagonist's rather casual manner of dressing (or in this case, not dressing) at home: "I hope we never get video-conferencing," she quipped.

For anybody whose life was punctuated by daily, traffic-clogged commutes across town, the message was intoxicating. You could do your job well, be recognized by your colleagues, and get "tons done," as the woman said, all in the terrycloth comfort of a bathrobe in your own home.

I still find the idea alluring, and it seems intuitive that many people would agree. Trading in a rush-hour commute for a calmer and possibly more effective way to work seems like a reasonable, even overwhelmingly advantageous, exchange. Ample evidence suggests that employers benefit, too, from allowing employees to work from home. Every published study about telework comes to the conclusion that productivity improves with teleworking. However, if one in five Americans occasionally participates in teleworking, that means four out of five don't. Why not?

Certainly, a large percentage of workers simply can't get their jobs done without physically traveling. Not every company or every boss is sold on the idea of conceding live oversight of their subordinates. Also, nobody is suggesting that we can get by without some amount of face-to-face interaction. We need to shake hands, smile and be smiled upon, laugh uproariously at spontaneous jokes, comfort colleagues who are facing difficult work situations, come up with great ideas over coffee in brainstorming sessions, toss yesterday's disappointing monthly sales report into the wastebasket with exaggerated fanfare for all to see, and negotiate prices and deals in person.

One of the unfortunate consequences of an overzealous promotion of telecommunications as a substitute for live human interaction is that we've burned out too many people with visions of a dark and moody future in which we interact only over a network. Not true, and it shouldn't be. I couldn't do what I do huddled alone over a glowing computer screen from my home office all day long, nor would I want to. Yet I can do some things very well without leaving my home. I could easily spend an entire day working from home—or maybe two or three days a week. Millions of other workers who are not currently listed in the current telecommuting estimates could, too.

Why aren't they? I think it has a lot to do with something that was tacitly promised in the MCI commercial. Or at least the vision that commercial represented. The woman in the commercial substituted an image, or a diagram, or some sort of designed graphic on the fly, zinging it almost instantly across the network to her colleagues, who quickly voiced their enthusiastic approval.

That particular piece of telecommunications wizardry, in truth, can't be performed by a majority of Americans from their homes today. Uploading even a garden-variety graphics file of 350 kilobytes in size takes time—about 50 seconds, on a 56-kbps dialup line. Certainly more time than the 30-second MCI commercial suggested.

For all you've heard about broadband communications to the home, the truth is that as of January 2003, according to the media measurement and research firm of Nielsen//NetRatings, narrowband, dialup users still compose the majority of the U.S. online population. Seventy-four million Americans continue to connect to the Internet from home using a connection technology that, at its finest hour, can wedge no more than 56 kbps down the network. (Thirty-three million Americans had broadband at the time of the study.) It's likely that at 56 kbps our revised graphic would putter along, taking nearly a minute to get where it's supposed to go. Remember, we're talking about a simple graphics file. For most Internet users, the idea of working with more elaborate formats, or in the more promising language of video, is unthinkable.

Unthinkable, that is, unless you're connected to a broadband network. A broadband connection would make everything we were promised in the MCI commercial a reality.

As reported previously, today's last-mile residential broadband connections can apply downstream data rates as high as 10 Mbps to residential appliances such as PCs. Upstream speeds tend to be slower, but there is an unmistakable trend toward symmetrical networks that will arm users with plenty of outbound data capacity.

Even today, most residential broadband users have enough capacity to do just about anything over the network: Sling video files, participate in live conferences, parcel out slide presentations, or anything else imaginable in a workplace environment. We are continuing to work on revisions to our core technologies and to our methods of distributing data that can bring even faster data rates and capabilities to the home.

Broadband already is stamping its imprint on the behaviors of teleworkers. A 2003 survey of 865 U.S. teleworkers by ITAC shows the presence of a broadband connection evokes meaningful increases in the use of digital work resources available to teleworkers (see Table 6-1).

Table 6-4   *What Teleworkers Do*

Activity	Dialup Users	Broadband Users
Access websites	61%	75%
Access Internet for information	54%	71%
Send large files	14%	36%
Use remote connection software	26%	34%
Do joint scheduling	20%	30%
Use groupware	17%	27%
Participate in telephone conferences	10%	16%
Use team project website	6%	14%
Work on the same document	5%	12%

Source: "Teleworking Comes of Age with Broadband: Telework America Survey 2002," International Telework Association & Council.

In Table 6-1, note the particularly wide disparity between dialup and broadband users in transmitting large files. Broadband has enabled teleworkers to do much more than simply communicate via e-mail or upload small text documents. Today, workers in industries ranging from graphic arts to audio recording can ply their trade from home.

One company arranges for advertising voice-overs to be produced by a network of freelancers whose homes are equipped with modern digital recording equipment. The firm e-mails scripts and instructions across the world to freelancers, who record the voice-overs and upload them via broadband networks within a few hours. The firm gets faster turnaround and access to a varied pool of voice-over talent, and it saves money because it doesn't have to build or staff a large recording facility.

Yet broadband promises more than just raw speed. Remember the description of the typical morning regimen in the office? To hear your voice-mail messages, you pick up the phone. To read e-mail, you turn to the computer. Here's another: Let's say you want to check on the stock market during the opening trading session. You flick on the television in the corner of your office, mute the volume, and keep an eye on the CNBC stock ticker crawling across the bottom of the screen. Now you're interacting with three different devices, and yet they're all connected to digital networks, and they're all processing the exact same fundamental substance of digital code.

Broadband is more than a way to distribute Internet pages and e-mail to your computer. Broadband networks are intended to render a new generation of commonality among our current trio of separately networked devices: the television set, the telephone, and the computer. That way, you can begin to do some truly interesting things in your job. It would be possible to sit in on a meeting, converse with the participants, speak up and be heard when you've got ideas to share, and sketch out an illustration or a flow chart of how you might put a plan into action—all without leaving your home, and all through a single network.

That's the type of connection needed to make telework an option for significantly more workers. The telework survey conducted by ITAC found that a lack of access to broadband technology was the single biggest barrier to more people teleworking. High-speed data connections are veritable staples of the modern office environment. Until people can match or exceed from their homes the type of broadband experience available in their offices, and until video, data, and voice content are able to travel together over a broadband IP network, the exhausting and environmentally painful commute to the office will continue to be a staple of worklife.

Even so, there is clearly a momentum toward telework, with large companies— including AT&T and Nortel—exhibiting fresh thinking about the merits of offsite work in which broadband plays an instrumental role. After launching a pilot telework program called HOMEbase in 1994, Nortel has fully embraced employee telework, with more than 14,000 employees working from home. Twenty-five percent of Nortel's teleworkers perform their jobs full-time from home, and the remaining 75 percent do at least some work from home. Telework is a growing force in government, too. The U.S. Office of Personnel Management (OPM) says the number of U.S. government employees who telework rose 21 percent to more than 90,000 as of November 2002. The federal government likes telework for the same reasons many corporations do: more productivity, cost savings, and environmental benefits. OPM, in fact, says it has been "relentless in our efforts to promote telework."

AT&T, which began exploring telework programs in 1989, reportedly has realized estimated savings of $25 million annually in real-estate costs thanks to virtual offices. The company's vice president of environment, health and safety, Dr. Braden Allenby, figures in another $100 million annually in incremental revenue thanks to improved productivity and employee retention. His research, cited in Table 6-2, shows six key major advantages of telecommuting cited by a majority of AT&T's teleworkers.

Table 6-5   *Advantages of Telework*

Benefit	Percentage of Employees Citing
Improves balance between work and family life	84%
Increases productivity	80%
Provides evidence company cares about people	78%
Helps company keep and attract the best people	77%
Gives employees more personal time by reducing commuting time	71%
Makes employees feel trusted	70%

Source: AT&T

The implications for a larger work-at-home workforce, or even a significant increase in the freedom to work from home at certain times, are profound. From a human standpoint, telecommuting often improves morale and productivity. It provides disabled people access to jobs and employment that might otherwise be elusive. It can reduce stress associated with commuting in the physical world. From an employer standpoint, telecommuting can help organizations attract talented workers tantalized by the idea of working from home or other locations of their choice.

One third of U.S. workers surveyed by the evangelistic Positively Broadband trade association have said they'd vote for telecommuting over a higher salary. Plus, telecommuting is a cost-saving alternative to sprawling offices that require heat, furniture, parking, and maintenance overhead, yet frequently do little more than to assemble workers into a physical space.

One obvious allure of telecommuting from the employer's vantage point is the tendency of telework to expand actual work hours for many employees. Legions of teleworkers talk enthusiastically about gladly trading in an hour of driving time for an extra hour of work time. The latest ITAC study attempts to put a dollar value on broadband-enabled teleworker productivity, based on the idea that teleworkers themselves believe their productivity has increased by an average of 33 percent since trading in their commute for a remote-work setting. That means an employee with an annual wage of $44,000 (and two weeks of vacation time annually) delivers $2,814 in annual productivity increase.

The Indianapolis pharmaceutical company Eli Lilly & Co. is a believer in the productivity benefits of telework, too. Lilly's formal telework program started as a way to help key employees achieve a better balance between their professional work and life outside the workplace. Lilly also liked what it saw from its teams of scientific writers, who, in a flextime telework pilot project, didn't miss a beat in submitting papers on time and without omissions.

As Eli Lilly's director of workforce planning said in the magazine *Information Week*, "Writers reported they were working just as hard and just as long, but they didn't feel overworked." Other telework studies support the worker-productivity theme. A study of American Express employees showed that teleworkers handled 26 percent more calls and produced 43 percent more business than their office-based colleagues, according to the Canadian Telework Association.

To be sure, many of the reports of enhanced employee productivity from telework are anecdotal rather than scientific, and some researchers, such as the University of Southern California's Ralph Westfall, question whether telework actually enhances productivity at all. The conclusion reached within one painstakingly impartial evaluation published by the U.S. Department of Labor is that although measuring telework productivity gains is difficult, "the subjective evaluations are nearly unanimous in suggesting at least modest productivity gains, on average." The author of this book would certainly agree: Nearly every page researched, submitted, edited, and ultimately produced was a product of at-home teleworking.

Productivity debates aside, the environmental benefits of telework are unmistakable. AT&T's Dr. Allenby calculates that in the year 2000, AT&T teleworkers alone withheld from the atmosphere some 50,000 tons of carbon dioxide emissions that otherwise would have been expelled as a byproduct of driving 110 million miles and consuming 5.1 million gallons of gasoline in the process. (One gallon of gasoline produces 19 pounds of carbon dioxide.) That's just for starters. More difficult to quantify are impacts such as reduced traffic and less demand for infrastructure. "Teleworking is thus not just an emissions reduction technology, but an energy efficiency technology as well, contributing to more efficient traffic patterns generally: Less traffic congestion makes everyone more efficient," Allenby said in testimony to the U.S. Congress.

The point is there are benefits on both sides of the table: Environmentalists and capitalists alike have things to admire in the broadband/telework arena. Surely, it's in nobody's interests to see the earth crumble under the weight of man's demands for resources. It is, scientists assure me, the only earth around.

Beaming Bits, Not Goods

There is another way to achieve a more balanced way of living, and using earth's resources, than employing political pressure to protect resources or to permit development. With a world population projected to swell to 9 billion by 2050, we have no choice but to teach new generations a new alphabet that can be used to replace the resource-taxing habits of our current, post-Industrial Age. Specifically, we can begin to curb our tendency to move things physically, and begin to think of inventive ways to move things digitally.

You can probably dream up as many examples as I can. One that comes to mind and seems to resonate with many people is that prerecorded video program housed on magnetic tape and sandwiched between two layers of industrially produced plastic. Enormously durable and lightweight, this thing we call the videocassette is, in all likelihood, destined to wind up someday in a trash heap. Maybe it contains a hit Hollywood movie or scenes from your four-year-old's backyard birthday party.

Let's go with the party example. You're anxious to share the day's glory with the child's grandmother, who lives hundreds of miles away. So you purchase an identical, but blank, videocassette, transfer the contents of your original to it, wrap it up with a cute greeting card in a padded envelope, and send it on a physical journey. Your package might be picked up on Monday by a local mail carrier, who likely drives a small delivery vehicle to a larger interstate delivery truck. The tape gets dumped off at a regional postal center, transferred, again by vehicle, to a secondary distribution outlet, and placed once again in a smallish van—all before it is tucked into your mother's mailbox in Indiana. The journey might take six or seven days, and at its conclusion your mother holds a physical replica of the same videocassette you started out with the preceding Sunday. Importantly, the value to your eager mother has nothing to do with the shiny black plastic surrounding the magnetic tape on which a recording of your party resides. She just wants to watch her grandchild blow out the candles.

This entire, complicated ritual could be replaced by an alternative in which you consumed neither the plastic and cardboard housing of a fresh videocassette nor the fuel, labor, and wear and tear of its physical delivery. The entire 12-minute recording could appear on your mother's television screen within minutes of its creation, accompanied by your live narration of key sequences ("…now watch Rover on the left corner of the screen…this is where he makes a dive for the cake…").

If only you had the right connections; in this case, a broadband appliance. It could be a broadband modem hooked to a PC, or a set-top device hooked to the TV, or a wholly new contraption, something called a residential gateway, which makes an in-home network for the PC, the TV, and many of the electronic appliances and gadgets in your home. This sort of communications gateway could snatch your video transmission, send it to your mother's electronic address, alert her that it had arrived, and display it on her command at the same time that she tuned into your live narration over the speaker.

The example reminds us why a converged broadband network—video, voice, and data—is so important. The cobbling together of separate networks is just too cumbersome for the average person to bear. Yes, today it is possible to digitize your 12-minute video and send it via e-mail over a dialup connection to your mother. If you're lucky, it should take no less than an hour or two to transmit. Of course, your mother must then possess the technical acumen to download the digital material you have sent her, summon and operate a computer application known as a decompression program, launch a separate program called a media player and, finally, call you via a separate telephone connection to describe the scenes she's viewing over her PC and ask for your commentary.

The idea that we have enough patience and expertise to engage in these varying levels of computer tomfoolery is silly. It should be no more difficult for your mother to watch her grandchild frolic in the backyard with friends than it is for her to watch the nightly news on over-the-air television. No special plug-in computer software, no dialing up to fetch a piece of e-mail, no separate phone call to connect to your voice.

The only way to achieve this sort of simplicity and ubiquity is to build a network over which the entire range of video, voice, and data content can flow. The brilliant pioneers who built the foundation for what we know as the Internet have created a vast mechanism for the exchange of information that abides by a common protocol. It is up to the emerging new broadband platforms to extend that foundation to the home. Using the Internet Protocol, we can fashion a network that delivers any manner of digitized content to the home.

The birthday video is just one example of how we can use the broadband network to exchange information more freely, in turn releasing tremendous pressure from our current system of moving things physically. Many organizations already have slashed billions of dollars in physical inventory costs by intelligently applying the capabilities of today's data networks to better track what's in stock. Examples of broadband's impact on business and the environment are plentiful. Rather than send employees around the country to keep tabs on its retail displays at stores, the athletic clothing manufacturer Nike Inc. now dispatches local residents to take photographs with digital cameras—and sling the results over a broadband network to the company headquarters.

Old habits do die hard, of course, and in the case of intellectual property, it is often comforting for suppliers to cloak their work in the protective garb of physical casings. It has long been the practice of software vendors, for example, to wrap their CD-ROM disks within elaborately illustrated cardboard boxes, sheathed in cellophane and that impossible-to-open tape, then sell them, unit by unit, as if they were more physical material than digital software code. Again, part of the practice is rooted in practicality. Until broadband's recent rise, it has been impractical to ask consumers to weather hours of download times to capture the application software they want. With broadband data transmission rates, a new opportunity has arisen for delivering software, recordings, video, photographs, and more.

The replacement of physical manufacturing and distribution with digital replication and distribution is an environmental benefit: less consumption of the planet's resources, less spewing of polluting emissions. Yet the bigger environmental impact of broadband is related to reducing traffic gridlock that increasingly haunts developed nations. It's about more than just pollution and resource consumption. Traffic increasingly gobbles up the precious resource of time.

An eye-opening observation from Harvard University's professor of public policy, Robert Putnam, notes that a long commute is among the biggest reasons for Americans' decreasing involvement in social groups such as school organizations, political parties, and churches. For every 10 minutes spent driving to work, Putnam observes, involvement in community affairs drops 10 percent.

A report on traffic congestion and commuting by the conservative Washington Family Council agrees with the idea that spending time in traffic erodes traditional values and life quality. "The long-term consequences of traffic reach far beyond simple economics," the report concluded. "It seeps into the foundation of society—people and their families." Of course, there's also the persistent fear of consuming more fuel than the earth ultimately has to give.

The dawning days of telecommuting, in fact, were rooted in concerns about energy consumption. It was during the 1970s' energy crisis and the U.S. government's embargo on Arab oil when the term telecommuting first came into vogue. Prompted by a government mandate to help employees pare their consumption of fuel, an unknown number of business workers toted heavy Teletype machines to their homes, plugged them into phone lines, and attempted to do their jobs.

More concerns about the environment sparked more government encouragement of telecommuting two decades later. In 1994, the U.S. government required businesses employing more than 100 people to develop plans for reducing employee commute time by 25 percent through car pools, public transportation, "or the most practical, cost-effective and popular option, telecommuting." The National Environmental Policy Institute even staged trial telecommuting programs in five large cities.

Telework loomed large, too, in the aftermath of the terrorist attacks against U.S. interests on Sept. 11, 2001. Thousands of workers displaced by the physical damage from the attacks were able to continue working from remote locations or from home thanks to the Internet, wireless technologies, and broadband connections.

No doubt cellular phones, e-mail, websites, and laptop computers have helped to contribute to the telecommute, or telework, evolution. So too have changing attitudes among corporations about decentralization, virtual work teams, and more permissive management philosophies. Still, only now do researchers envision a truly remarkable change in the way professional people work. Global broadband connections, wired or wireless, represent the spark that can ignite the real progression in telework. It's the presence, or lack, of broadband connectivity that often spells the difference in whether telework works. "Our employee research has shown that lack of broadband into the home is the top barrier to increased participation," said AT&T's telework guru Allenby. "Lack of high-speed access to the inter/intranet draws workers back into the office for the sake of productivity, in this age of larger and larger computer files and applications such as video conferencing."

However, the expansion of broadband availability portends a day when some of the impositions of the Industrial Age give way. Ironically, we might just end up where we started—with a more natural blend of work life and home life. "It was only with the advent of the manufacturing economy of the Industrial Revolution that workers began leaving their homes in droves each day, assembling together for employment, then returning home," observed Allenby. "Before the Industrial Revolution, the lines between work and family and education and entertainment were blurry. Everything blended just a little bit, because all activity in an agrarian economy tended to occur around the homesite. Then, we drew clear, Industrial Age lines between everything, and spent time, energy, and natural resources moving ourselves back and forth to keep work and family and education separate. Now, as we move into the information age, it seems telework is actually a return to a more organic way of balancing work and family."

For years, broadband evangelists have searched for the elusive killer application that might unleash even greater momentum in broadband adoption rates. Maybe the real allure of broadband isn't on-demand music access, streaming videos, or e-mail that talks to you. Maybe it's eroding the stress of traffic gridlock that will be the siren song of the new broadband age.

Summary

In summary, one of broadband's more alluring features is to change the fundamental character of work. In an information age, knowledge workers can often conduct much or all of their work from remote locations, particularly if they're outfitted with high-speed broadband networks, and the electricity to power them. As teleworking increases, it becomes increasingly critical to engineer our broadband networks and electrical grid systems to assure a constant and reliable supply of electrical energy—the broadband equivalent of gasoline for the automobile. Telework, already growing in popularity, seems destined to thrive in a broadband civilization, potentially relieving millions of people of the Industrial Age imposition of having to physically travel in order to perform work. Anecdotal but persuasive reports about productivity benefits, coupled with obvious environmental benefits and improvements in employment opportunities for those with disabilities, all point to a more prominent role for broadband in the new world of work that awaits.

CHAPTER 7

BROADBAND CONTENT

FOR YEARS, THE PEOPLE WHO RUN Major League Baseball have fretted that slow-moving games are turning fans off, hurting attendance, and depressing TV ratings. Baseball's ruling legislators have asked pitchers to speed up their warm-up sessions and commanded umpires to pick up the pace. The new rules have succeeded in trimming several minutes from the average game's length, and today the final out is usually recorded in just under three hours.

Imagine if a time-pressed fan could enjoy a start-to-finish game in only 20 minutes.

Impossible? Not with broadband. Thanks to a combination of content and technology, some baseball fans can turn on their broadband connections and watch an entire game in less than half an hour.

It's a novel content idea available only over high-speed broadband Internet networks. Starting with the 2003 season, Major League Baseball has begun offering a condensed version of games over the league's mlb.com website. Editors pare down the action by eliminating every pitch that doesn't result in a hit, run, or out. Purists might protest, but these games, streamed over the Internet at a speed of about 300 kbps, deliver a sort of "baseball-light" version of the game.

Condensing baseball games isn't the only thing mlb.com offers over a broadband content option that's available for subscription fees ranging from $11.95 to $19.95 per month. Fans with high-speed connections can watch entire games live, select nightly highlights on demand, watch player interviews on demand, and more.

The condensed presentations deliver a terrific example of the possibilities of broadband content. Rather than serve merely as another outlet for the same content available elsewhere (on radio or television, for example), broadband allows producers to expand into new and different experiences. Condensed baseball games "satisfy an unmet need, somewhere between full-length games at the ballpark and nightly highlight shows," says Ian McKerlich, senior director of Broadband Strategy & Business for RealNetworks, the Seattle, Washington-based company that is assisting MLB in shaping and delivering its broadband content.

RealNetworks is a good example of the broadband ripple effect. As broadband adoption rates grow in the U.S., Europe, Asia, and elsewhere, the investment appeal of producing content for the broadband sector increases. Granted, nobody is getting rich yet, and some of the early broadband content entrants such as NBC's snap.com broadband portal and the experimental television service pseudo.com have been shut down. However, there is a big economic difference between pursuing a broadband content play today—when the worldwide user base exceeds 40 million—versus four years ago, when the potential audience was less than 7 million households. Although producers still must bear substantial bandwidth costs to get their content distributed to users, scale economics are now within striking distance for profit-minded broadband content producers.

The Walt Disney Co., for example, has begun to sense a sort of tipping point for broadband content. With the U.S. residential broadband base surpassing 20 million households, a new opportunity is at hand, says Larry Shapiro, executive vice president of the Walt Disney Internet Group (WDIG). "Twenty million is sort of the magic point in the U.S.," Shapiro says, "where you start getting beyond your early adopters who wanted speed just for speed's sake. Now you're getting to an audience that wants to find some value, some entertainment, or some utility in the experience that can be delivered by broadband."

Disney has been among the more active broadband content developers, with special programming ranging from on-demand news reports from its ABC News division to live, interactive multiplayer games over its own content sites to instant-play sports clips and on-demand highlights over its ESPN.com website. With ABC News, broadband users can summon news reports at will from a menu of available stories. Those interested purely in news from the Middle East, for example, can select relevant reports uniquely. Extra content comes in the form of textual information at the bottom of the screen offering expanded information and links to additional online sources.

Furthermore, even deeper broadband content is available online. ABC News makes available to broadband users interview footage and content that was left on the proverbial cutting-room floor of the network's nightly newscast or ABC's popular *20/20* news program. "In the case of Barbara Walters interviews on *20/20*, where we showed only 30 minutes on the air, we'll have the full interview available," says Shapiro. "It's interesting both for the time-shifting element, plus the fact that you see all the bonus material you wouldn't otherwise see."

In addition to repurposing material originally produced for traditional mediums, Disney's companies have invented original broadband content such as the animated multiplayer kids game, Toontown, in which players assume the persona of cartoon characters and defend the populace against evil-doers. The three-dimensional world of Toontown is designed graphically to get the most out of today's high-speed broadband Internet connections. "It's too heavy and too rich to play in a narrowband environment," says Shapiro. "It's something that really showcases what speed brings to you."

Still, Shapiro knows that Toontown and other new incarnations of broadband content go beyond flashy data pyrotechnics. Broadband games such as Toontown are also about interacting, meeting friends, and developing a sense of community. "The concept is to design something that both takes advantage of and requires the strength of a broadband connection," says Shapiro.

The broadband content game is still young. Although the historic tendency of Internet users to shirk paying for content remains a tough obstacle, a growing number of indicators suggest the right combination of content, price, and convenience will draw paying subscribers into the fold.

Content is important to the growth and appeal of the broadband data category. Until now, the main appeal of a broadband residential data connection has been a better, faster Internet experience. Broadband has undoubtedly improved this core experience by delivering faster web page load times and crisper overall responsiveness, but these attributes alone are unlikely to sway a mass conversion from narrowband connections. Richer experiences are the goal, and many providers who work a broad spectrum of entertainment, commerce, and information believe broadband has the potential not just to improve, but to transform the Internet into something new and more meaningful.

Already within the U.S., according to the Arbitron Co., more than 100 million people over the age of 12 have sampled video and audio content over the Internet, and 47 million Americans — one in five — are regular patrons, having watched or listened to Internet content within the past month. Again, broadband inspires more usage, as 25 percent of those with broadband connections have watched or listened to Internet broadcasts within the last week, versus just 12 percent of dialup users, according to Arbitron's 2003 report titled, "Media Research Internet and Multimedia 10 Study: The Emerging Digital Consumer."

Real money is now being spent to support more elaborate and fulfilling content across the Internet. If the trend continues, it's likely to lead to a more stratified Internet — one in which premium content is available only to fee-paying subscribers, and free content exists only as long as providers care to subsidize it, or ample advertising revenue continues to fund it.

RealNetworks is one of the new cadres of fee-charging broadband content providers and aggregators. In 2000, when the dot.com sector was imploding and doom and gloom seemed to prevail over the entire "new media" category, Real's founder Rob Glaser staked the company's future on broadband. Observing the steady increases in broadband-connected households, Glaser launched a subscription-based business to deliver video and audio content over the web, despite vocal objections from some of his own colleagues.

Today, Real's subscription services include a broad array of content, including video news reports and documentaries from ABC, programming from more than 3000 radio stations, live sports events, video games, and more. So far, there is good progress to report. As of mid-2003, more than one million subscribers pay an average of $8.50 a month to enjoy Real's wide range of news, music, entertainment, and sports programs. The quick math indicates a rough estimate of $102 million in annualized revenue. That's hardly the torrent of billions of dollars that analysts believe could some day accrue to new forms of broadband content, but it's a start, and the habit is building. On a given evening, several thousand will tune into baseball live-game telecasts or condensed-version games, and tens of thousands more will catch up with news documentaries, music videos, and more.

Because it has populated the Internet world with computer servers that optimize audio and video for the web, and because it distributes millions of copies of a widely used application that allows users to play streaming media, Real has constructed an infrastructure that serves as a good barometer of activity in the broadband media segment. One clear trend—thanks to broadband—is an increase in the amount and duration of video offered over the Real subscription services. "We're shifting more from audio-centric programming to video-centric programming, and we're seeing the duration of the video getting longer," says Real's McKerlich. "It used to be, at 56 kbps, it was acceptable to watch a news story for a few minutes...now with broadband data rates, through our partnership with ABC News, we have a 24/7 news product on our platform."

The explosion in audio and video over the Internet is happening because broadband data rates today support acceptable-to-good video quality, depending on factors such as connection speed, media compression/decompression techniques, and the performance of the backbone network over which requested streams or downloads travel. Broadband is the much anticipated engine poised to propel entertainment and information delivered either via download—the capturing of data files to a storage device for later playback—or via streaming media, a technology that relies on faster data connections to shuttle video and audio feeds that play immediately as they are received.

Streaming media content starts as stored material that's delivered through a system consisting of an encoder, a server, and a player—the former two in the network, and the latter inside your computer. Unlike a download, which captures an entire media file all at once for later playback, a streaming event is a continuous event. It starts when you point your mouse to the Play button and click, and ends when the event is complete, or when you click Stop.

Streaming media is a complicated and demanding application that depends mightily on broadband. In the narrowband environment, unfortunately, many streaming applications crumble under the strain of limited bandwidth, displaying themselves in the form of jittery or unfathomable video images, and audio that starts and halts in a sort of unbearable tedium. Early explorers of the streaming media world will recognize a big contrast between video quality viewed over today's broadband access networks and the relatively horrific quality of postage-stamp sized, stuttering, and unreliable video feeds that preceded it. Audio content quality, too, has improved dramatically, and broadband's growing customer base is helping radio stations reach wider and more dispersed audiences by porting their programming over the web.

Even naysayers must now recognize that a continued evolution in streaming media technology has yielded impressive results. In 2003, the sports-content company ESPN introduced a proprietary software application, ESPN Motion, that allows broadband users to download video assets onto their computers immediately, without any of the preplay buffering routines that sometimes delay streaming media requests. The effect is elegantly simple, not unlike turning on a television set and being greeted immediately with moving images.

ESPN is integrating more video into its site because, increasingly, its visitors can accommodate high bit-rate media. John Skipper, an ESPN executive vice president, is a publishing veteran who is at home in a world of rich graphic design, typography, and photographs. When he joined the ESPN.com group in January 2000, Skipper was frustrated by the limitations of narrowband connections, which prevented ESPN.com from making its website as attractive and interesting as he wanted it. Skipper's reaction was to forge ahead anyway for a broadband world he felt certain would arrive.

"I just said, 'You know what, we're going to make a bet that over time, people's connections will get bigger, fatter, and broader. We're going to program a better-looking site and, overall, we'll be better off if we satisfy people with better connections,'" Skipper said. It turns out he was right. Today the percentage of visitors to the ESPN.com site who have broadband connections has soared from about 33 percent in 2000 to 82 percent in 2003, thanks to a combination of growing residential and workplace broadband availability.

One reality check to report is that despite vast improvements in the ability to shuttle video and audio content along the Internet, rare is the user who would regard Internet-delivered video to a computer as superior to the picture that appears on the living room TV set from conventional broadcasting means. The current video applications that draw interest via broadband IP networks tend to be novel or compelling not because of their picture quality but because they deliver some attribute unavailable over conventional television broadcasting. It might be an interactive element, such as the ability to summon today's top new clips on demand, or it might be a content element, such as the ability to watch programs (or baseball games, for that matter) that aren't otherwise available on television. The day when traditional television flows to us over the Internet is a long way off. Still, video is beginning to course through the broadband IP world in interesting ways.

Types of Content

Content is potentially the biggest driver of further residential broadband penetration. One of the reasons broadband's availability so far exceeds the number of people who have chosen to subscribe has to do with what the network delivers. We are an easily spoiled society. If all we get for $40 a month is merely a faster rendition of a web page, broadband connections might never increase to a point of critical mass. Millions of Internet users still rely on the network primarily to read largely textual web pages, to dish out e-mails or to chat over instant-messaging networks, and these activities are certainly well-served by standard narrowband Internet connections.

So what might attract the next 10, 20, 30 million users to the broadband experience? The same thing that attracts people to go to the movies, buy recorded music, enjoy books and magazines, watch television shows, and buy up all the tickets to hit Broadway shows: great stories, great performances, great content. Plus, something that broadband is uniquely poised to do: allow individuals to produce their own content and interact with one another in new ways.

Broadband content spans a wide range of applications that serve different purposes. Some are related to core Internet functionality—faster downloads, for example—and others are truly novel approaches to bringing creative works in front of audiences. Here are some of the more interesting content possibilities enabled by broadband.

User-Generated Content

User-generated content doesn't mean every broadband household is hereby challenged to throw a feature-length original movie up on the network. There are many ways in which users might begin to produce their own content, some of it personal and intended for microaudiences, and some of it meant for wider attention and appreciation.

Evidence of this transformation from consumer-to-producer is already at work. One well-publicized example occurred in 2001, when an unknown apprentice released unto the digital ether an unauthorized but adroitly edited variation of the George Lucas movie *The Phantom Menace*, part of the popular *Star Wars* film series. Using inexpensive but powerful digital-editing software, the interloper created his own interpretation of the movie, mainly by deleting many of the scenes in which a not-universally beloved character known as Jar Jar Binks appeared. The Jar Jar-free version, dubbed *Stars Wars 1.1*, quickly found its way around the Internet, where an unknown number of fans downloaded and, presumably, watched the edited movie. It had been carefully sliced into two 100-megabyte (MB) files, each of which would have taken about eight minutes to capture over a speedy download connection speed of around 1.5 Mbps. (In the slow-moving narrowband world, of course, the rogue movie never would have seen the light of day.)

True, the renegade *Menace* version and the various offspring it inspired raised serious legal and copyright issues, and I'm not suggesting the role of a broadband network is to inspire unauthorized duplication and manipulation of another person's intellectual property.

Quite the contrary. Numerous nettlesome issues must be sorted out concerning copyright at large in the digital age; broadband brings even more urgency to them. A study funded by the Motion Picture Association of America estimates between 400,000 and 600,000 movies are illegally downloaded every day. The point is that, with broadband, we are putting a powerful publishing and distribution mechanism into the hands of a much wider populace of users, and broadband is certain to invite a throng of creative people to use it in inventive and unexpected ways.

More common than editing movies and illegally slinging them across the network is another sort of content creation that should flourish under broadband. The broadband network offers an ideal *tableau* for turning the world's population of amateur photographers and videographers into publishers who share their work with people on the other end of the line. The prevalence of affordable digital cameras for still photography and videography makes it easy for people to capture images in a fundamental digital form that allows for IP network delivery.

Already, it is common practice for enthusiastic parents to zing photos of their newborn babies to friends and relatives within a day of two of the big event. The next step is to treat digital video in the same way. The proud patriarch of the 1950s who gathered neighbors in the basement to watch home movies of the family trip to the Grand Canyon hasn't disappeared; he's just changed his medium of expression to videos sent via broadband.

Personalized and niche-targeted video is the sleeping giant of broadband content. From home movies to mini-epics conceived and distributed by budding Steven Spielbergs, broadband offers a forum for video delivery and distribution we've never seen before. The range of ideas is literally without limit. A Toronto-based company, FuneralCast.com, has set up shop to produce broadband video coverage of funerals, allowing bereaved relatives and friends unable to attend in person to share the experience of paying their respects. Since its launch in August of 2002, more than 30,000 viewers have watched ceremonies, which are available only to authorized visitors on a password-protected basis.

Of course, as with most new media categories, the role of adult-oriented content can't be ignored. One sexually oriented website, danni.com, generates more than $10 million annually by delivering streamed videos to more than 30,000 fee-paying broadband subscribers.

Broadband's ability to support video bit streams isn't all that's required for fostering wider acceptance of Internet video, however. Managing the distribution of video requires an administrative system for controlling and parceling out legitimate rights to view and/or manipulate material. So-called digital-rights management tools that dictate the terms under which user-generated video can be viewed and authorized are a work in progress, although a fairly impressive list of companies and organizations are working hard on these issues now.

Then, there's the monitoring aspect of broadband video—the opportunity to attach an inexpensive web camera to the network and keep tabs on your home, your child's schoolroom, even how your pets behave while you're away. For the cost of around $200 in web cameras and related software, broadband users can attach simple webcams to their network and keep watch over their homes or properties while traveling or at work. (Here, again, security bears some attention. Without effective firewall and security systems, these same images could be viewed by others.)

Finally, video promises to inject further momentum into the category of e-commerce—the business of selling everything from software to model railroad parts online. In 2003, consumer buying over the Internet is expected to approach $100 billion. E-commerce will embrace broadband for the same reason that Hollywood has: It enriches the user experience.

Meg Whitman, the chief executive officer of the hugely popular eBay service, which allows users to sell and purchase merchandise in a digital-age auction setting, has pointed to broadband as a big contributor to growth. Users can better display their wares by attaching not just static photos but full-motion video that showcases everything from vintage automobiles to barely used home-exercise equipment. Plus, broadband's faster response times and always-on connectivity make it easier to browse through merchandise and place orders swiftly.

As the broadband age gathers steam, video—commercial, homemade, and everything in-between—will be one of its most forceful engines.

Again, broadband isn't reinventing the Internet; it's just making the Internet work better. Over today's prevalent narrowband networks, video poses huge challenges. Even when run through rigorous squeeze-and-compress regimens designed to reduce video to the smallest possible data sizes, the medium taxes the narrowband access network to a point where the end experience rarely is worth the effort. Sending your home movie to grandma over a narrowband Internet connection is all but futile. Broadband, which spans not just a fat pipe, but the servers, receiving devices, and managed networks in-between, enables you to accomplish the feat with relative ease.

Entertainment on Broadband

In the commercial realm, more and more content meant to ride the fast waves of the broadband network is beginning to percolate. In August 2001, a band of big-name Hollywood movie studios (Metro-Goldwyn-Mayer Studios, Paramount Pictures, Sony Pictures Entertainment, Universal Studios, and Warner Bros.) launched a joint venture designed to digitize movies and make them available—conveniently and legally—over the Internet for around $2.99 to $4.99 apiece.

The announcement marked the first official embrace of the broadband IP network by the world's biggest moviemakers, which heretofore have been worried sick about the threat posed by unauthorized distribution over the Internet. The venture—called Movielink—gives Hollywood a chance to experiment a bit. Studios can figure out the right ways both to encrypt movies so they can't readily be duplicated, and to sort through copyright and legal clearances that should allow broadband to emerge as a valid medium for home entertainment. Movielink is sort of a video-rental store on the web, available only to broadband users. (A settings-detection engine appearing at Movielink's home page warns would-be visitors if they lack the requisite bandwidth to use the service. The minimum is 128 kbps.)

Others have followed suit. In November 2002, the pay-TV company Starz Encore Group announced a subscription movies-on-demand service that allows broadband users to download mainstream Hollywood movies (such as *Kate and Leopold* and *Black Hawk Down*) and view them at their convenience. The chairman of Starz Encore Group, John Sie, notes it can take an hour or more to download a movie that has been encoded at a high-quality bit rate. However, he suggests that amount of time compares favorably to the typical driving time it takes to rent a DVD or videocassette version of the same product—and return it to the store within a few days.

True enough, after-hours downloads are becoming a ritual for consumers who enjoy movies and TV shows over their PCs. With always-on broadband connections, it's fairly simple to capture files measured in the hundreds of megabits while users doze peacefully in the meantime.

PC Versus TV

It's difficult to think of an issue in the media ecosystem that has consumed so many hours of studied what-ifs and lofty reasoning as the infamous PC versus TV debate. For a decade or more, media theorists have swapped predictions and wrestled over the idea of whether some sort of truce is at hand between the PC and the TV set, or whether the two are destined to forever maintain their separate roles within the household.

It is true that because the vast majority of appliances connected to today's residential broadband IP networks are computers, not TV sets, most broadband content tends to be viewed, or listened to, over the PC. Conversely, most traditional broadcast television programming tends to be watched on the TV set. Even though a growing number of television signals are digital, they're cloaked in a different sort of digital format—MPEG-2—than the packets of data that flow within the Internet Protocol over our broadband Internet networks. Thus, most of us continue to have two prevailing information appliances using two different digital delivery formats in the home.

Eventually, we might stop caring about this dichotomy entirely, as two factors come more prominently into play.

First, a wider variety of appliances—neither PCs entirely, nor TVs entirely—will find their way into our lives. At one extreme, consider the Samsung Corp.'s new Internet-enabled refrigerator. Not only does it keep food cold, it includes a monitor and keypad enabling users to surf the web or to watch television. Connected via either a wireless network or direct broadband, it's emblematic of a new breed of connected appliances that roam free of traditional definitions. Alluring, too, are new devices such as photo frames or picture cubes that collect and display digital images from an IP stream. While you curl up on the couch with your hot tea, you can enjoy watching a catalog of family photos magically appear, disappear, and reappear at intervals you choose within your broadband-enabled photo display device. Finally, flat-panel screens that can display traditional TV broadcasts or be connected to broadband IP networks tend to unravel the distinctions between a TV screen and a PC screen. The dispersal of broadband IP devices throughout the home—and even beyond the home, thanks to wireless networking—tends to make some of our worry about the PC versus the TV moot.

Second (and further down the road), wider adoption of in-home broadband networks, or "home premises networks," could ultimately erode the PC versus TV debate. Instead, media content ranging from simple web pages to full-blown DVD movies will flow across a common broadband platform, accessible to any and all devices that speak its language of open standards. If you prefer to enjoy it from the wide-screen, high-definition television monitor, or you'd rather watch from a handheld wireless screen in the backyard, it is your choice.

In the meantime, be aware that we're years away from any meaningful conversion of television signals and Internet content to a common delivery platform. Instead, two different markets are likely to coexist; one optimized for PC and IP appliances; the other optimized for the television set.

Downloading large media files, such as movies, TV shows, and music, is impractical without broadband. Over a dialup connection delivering a sustained data rate of 56 kbps, it would take more than an hour of download time to capture the contents of a typical music CD. A broadband connection operating at 1 Mbps, in contrast, would digest the album in less than five minutes. Movies are another story. Movies pose particular challenges because the file sizes are enormous compared with music. The average file size of a movie available for download from the Movielink service ranges from 600 MB to 1 gigabit (Gb), meaning that even at a sustained connection rate of 1 Mbps, it takes close to two hours to download the file. At a narrowband connection rate of 56 kbps, it would take at least 23 hours.

That said, news about a tacit endorsement of broadband by the kingpins of Tinseltown is particularly welcome given the tense history between digital networks and content owners. Until recently, litigation, not innovation, has been the watchword as enthusiastic broadband network users met up with resistance from the world's media titans. Many of the global entertainment companies that distribute recorded music, movies, and TV shows are understandably wary about digital delivery over broadband networks. Fundamentally, digital media represents a piracy threat like the world has never seen. Without adequate piracy-prevention measures, creative content that's turned into digital code is easy to copy and distribute, and it usually renders superb reproduction quality. Movielink uses a digital-rights technology from Microsoft that not only encrypts downloaded movies to guard against unauthorized distribution, but administers the terms of their rental. Movielink users can store their downloaded titles for up to 30 days, but within 24 hours of hitting the Play button, downloaded Movielink movies disappear from a user's computer.

Hollywood has reason to be cautious about allowing digital versions of its content to course through the Internet. The most notorious poster-child for a nervous entertainment industry was Napster, the file-sharing service that rose to enormous popularity among music fans in 2000-2001, but was extinguished under legal pressure from record companies. (Major record labels won a legal victory when a federal judge grounded Napster by ordering it to suspend its free-music sharing system in July 2001, until all copyrighted music was removed.) Napster might have been vanquished, but copycat services, such as the popular Kazaa and Morpheus file-sharing networks, continue to thrive. In fact, they're more popular than ever.

Kazaa and its ilk are peculiarly amorphous beasts. They don't fit the typical definition of a company or an enterprise. Instead, they're loosely orchestrated arrangements of computers connected to other computers that, taken together, made it easy to sort through, snatch, and possess a piece of digitally recorded music or video. This activity occurs much to the lament of a recorded music industry that has seen U.S. unit shipments of recorded CDs and tapes slide by 26 percent, from 1.16 billion in 1999 to 860 million in 2002, according to the Recording Industry Association of America (RIAA).

Using a digital file format called MP-3 (short for MPEG-3), music fans continue to download songs at a pace that has sent shockwaves through an entire industry. Whereas prerecorded CD sales are down, sales of blank CDs—suitable for storing both legally and illegally downloaded media content—were up 40 percent in 2002, to 1.7 billion units. In the meantime, users have snatched more than 230 million downloads from the Kazaa file-sharing service. At the current pace, the RIAA estimates Kazaa adds 13 million new members a month—or 270 every minute.

The broadband age will require content owners to come up with thoughtful ways to present and secure content over the network. These new delivery systems need to be so easy to use, affordable, and inviting that the idea of illegally pirating material seems hopelessly cumbersome by comparison. Piracy won't be solved by litigation or technology alone, but also by convenience: Legitimate music download services are tiny by comparison to the Kaazas of the world, but they work better, perform more reliably, and ultimately need to prevail if a workable economic system for creative content is to continue.

Latter-day, legitimate variations of music download services are already cropping up. The America Online AOL MusicNet, musicmatch, Full Audio, pressplay, and RealNetworks' Rhapsody allow registered subscribers to roam through thousands of tracks, view artist profiles, program their own radio stations, and legally download songs with modest playback restrictions (for example, some can be stored only on a local computer). Apple Computer's iTunes retail web storefront lets users choose from hundreds of thousands of fully authorized songs from major recording artists. Selected songs can be downloaded and burned to a compact disc for just 79 cents each. RealNetworks has launched a similar music storefront. Bear in mind that neither is described as a broadband service, but both work better and faster over a broadband connection by offering swift downloads.

Playing with Broadband

Another content category that stands out early on in the broadband age is video gaming. Once deemed the playground of adolescent boys, gaming has become big business. Americans now spend more money on video games than they spend going to the movies—and broadband connectivity could usher in still another dramatic growth spurt. We've started to see a groundswell of interest in online gaming communities and services.

As of mid-2003, Sony's EverQuest online multiplayer game was routinely drawing more than 100,000 simultaneous users. EverQuest allows gamers to delve into a virtual 3-D fantasy world that seems to truly come alive on the screen, especially with the aid of a high-powered broadband connection. Players assume the role of game characters who barter and trade, battle one another, and otherwise interact through a huge online community that, for many, is an intoxicating journey into a fictional realm. Through March 2003, 430,000 subscribers had signed up, paying Sony around $12.95 per month (after purchasing a $50 game CD) to roam the fantasy world.

Broadband contributes to the online gaming phenomenon because most games are extremely sensitive to response time. Even delays measured in milliseconds can have discernable (and usually negative) consequences for players. Some game industry analysts blamed the absence of a critical mass of broadband subscribers for contributing to the doom of Sega's 1999-2000 Dreamcast video game platform, which sought to involve players in online games.

Dreamcast might have been ahead of its time. The unmistakable trend under way now is to hook up broadband networks to video game consoles themselves—rather than PCs loaded with game software—so online game enthusiasts can take advantage of the richer graphics and, in most cases, faster processors embedded in the latest generation of game systems from Sony, Microsoft, and Nintendo—the three big market leaders.

Better gaming action, better graphics, and more interaction with other players on the network are certain to captivate more and more enthusiasts. "Online console gaming over broadband will change the face of video games forever," says Robbie Bach, architect of Microsoft's Xbox gaming platform "Broadband online video games will have as dramatic an impact on the industry for the current generation of games as the move from 2-D to 3-D graphics did for the last generation."

In short, broadband injects new life into the multiplayer games category, and more game companies are adapting their content to suit an online broadband community. For Disney's Internet Group, the timing of Toontown in 2002 was anything but coincidental. "We're getting to a critical mass in broadband," said group president Steve Wadsworth in a front-page Wall Street Journal article about the product.

Companies that make games are excited about what broadband can do in other ways, too. Some games are outfitted with voice-communication capability so players can talk to one another during the action, rather than rely on text messages, as is currently commonplace.

Online games could be big business. One firm that follows the category, Datamonitor, projects the online video game market will grow to $2.9 billion in 2005 from an estimated $670 million in 2002.

Broadband Telephony

There's another content category that deserves attention in a broadband context: your voice.

Although slow to develop, the market for Voice over Internet Protocol (VoIP) services is beginning to blossom. Originally viewed as an experimental way to save money on long-distance phone calls, VoIP now describes an entire range of applications that depend on reliable network connections and the conversion of voice conversations to digital packets that ride along the Internet.

Some of the new voice applications emerging for broadband IP networks are truly alluring. With broadband IP telephone services, you can work all sorts of magic. You can set up a temporary telephone line and number in the spare bedroom when your friend from Toledo visits for the weekend. Then, you can make it disappear just as readily when he leaves. You can, for the first time in a practical application, tie your voice conversations to video pictures and images. Yes, variations of the famous AT&T Picturephone that captivated onlookers at the 1964 World's Fair are on the way, thanks to broadband.

VoIP is gaining traction in Japan, particularly, where more than two million people have Internet phones tied to VoIP technology. The main provider, a joint venture of Yahoo! Japan and Softbank, has used VoIP as a centerpiece of a DSL-based broadband service. Getting VoIP telephone service costs about $10 per month extra for those who have the DSL service. With no per-minute charges for calls that travel purely over the Internet, Softbank/Yahoo is a bargain compared with Nippon Telephone & Telegraph, Japan's principal phone carrier.

In the U.S., the most active provider is Vonage, which offers a $40-a-month service including unlimited domestic calls plus low-cost international calls. For $25, Vonage customers get up to 500 minutes of long-distance calls—more than most customers ever use. In addition to these more visible consumer services, many companies with international offices already routinely use VoIP to connect distant offices at low costs.

Broadband is an enabler of VoIP content largely because of the reliability of broadband connections versus dialup Internet access. Voice packets actually consume very little bandwidth; 64 kbps in each direction is the standard for what we know as voice-grade telephone service. However, voice conversations are extremely demanding on the performance front, with sensitivity to network delay and occasional packet loss that other applications can more easily withstand. The higher bit rate of a broadband connection alleviates the delay and packet loss associated with a lower-speed IP connection.

Telephone service is generally considered a necessity, and is often described as a lifeline service in its elemental form. Whether consumers in large numbers will flock to Internet-based telephony is questionable. Most telephone networks in advanced economies work well and are affordable. Yet growing comfort with the reliability of broadband networks should help VoIP gain credibility and market presence, and the combination of lower calling costs plus added service benefits could make VoIP a bigger contributor to the broadband content mix going forward.

Meet the New Internet(s)

A final trend worth noting as broadband-specific content evolves is the idea that what we've become accustomed to as the Internet—one singular content repository available to all—will likely morph into a more disjointed collective of individual, private networks. They might all use the language and technical standards that have helped the Internet flourish, but these networks will deliver unique content to their own subscribers.

It is also likely they'll employ edge-of-the-network computer caches that store applications and content closer to the end-user, thus reducing congestion associated with the public Internet. This sort of privatized approach has already been adopted by certain broadband providers including the Road Runner high-speed Internet service developed by a unit of AOL Time Warner, and more recently by America Online's broadband service itself, which delivers a broad range of member-only content. For example, in July 2003, fans of the TV series *Friends* could glimpse a sneak preview of the final episode exclusively from AOL Broadband. Various DSL service providers from time to time have announced similar content initiatives, angling to deliver something fresh and unique, other than merely delivering high-speed access to the public Internet.

In many cases, the companies that own the transmission facilities for broadband access networks have economic advantages in delivering their own unique content, and might begin to offer proprietary services and applications as a way to enhance their broadband offerings and preserve their customer base.

Unquestionably, broadband promises new levels of convenience, control, and choice in what movies we watch and what musicians we listen to, but its biggest appeal, from a content perspective, might turn out to be the chance to look inward—to ourselves and our loved ones, in ways we're only beginning to imagine. The ability of a young, working mother to watch her toddler doze off to sleep from a hotel room 600 miles away is a powerful argument for maintaining a broadband network connection. Try telling a proud uncle who is about to watch a video clip of his niece reciting her wedding vows that broadband isn't worth it.

Summary

The fact that big forces in films, music, and games are lined up to take advantage of the broadband platform should help propel the next layer of broadband adoption. A similar uptick occurred in the cable television sector during the early 1980s, when the medium morphed from an outpost that retransmitted over-the-air TV stations to a home for uncut, commercial-free movies and recognizable stars. What was once sold as basic cable got augmented with premium channels, such as HBO and Showtime. The logic holds that broadband Internet service as we know it today—faster Internet access— could morph into basic broadband, with premium content stacked on top. Broadband content will operate as an on-demand medium, allowing busy consumers to fit programming into their schedules and lifestyles. People will watch, read, or listen to what they want, when they want.

Before this can truly occur, content producers must become comfortable with the security of the network. The good news is, broadband is now attracting serious interest—and serious money—from an entertainment and content community that once shunned the idea of digital distribution. Entertainment, music, and games won't be the only forces that drive more people to sign up for broadband connections, but they'll surely contribute to the momentum.

CHAPTER 8

BROADBAND EVERYWHERE

TODAY, EVEN AS BROADBAND networks proliferate, a majority of the residential population within developed countries doesn't currently subscribe to broadband service, or physically cannot receive broadband because the delivery agents haven't built or upgraded their facilities. In rural areas where low housing densities make it difficult, if not impossible, to earn a return on investment from building broadband networks, residents are at risk of being left behind in the broadband age, furthering the so-called digital divide that concerns many information age policy makers. In short, although broadband has grown and continues to grow rapidly, the sheer potential of the medium leaves us wanting more presence, faster.

When we praise the fast growth rates that have resulted in broadband reaching nearly 20 percent of U.S. households, for example, we routinely tiptoe around the fact that 80 percent of the country remains unmoved by the broadband argument.

Two forces need to be in play to change this. One is the "pull" of more alluring content or applications, coupled with increasingly affordable pricing that will sway more people to exchange narrowband networks for broadband. The other is the "push" of continued investment that will put even better broadband connectivity at the doorstep of every household—much in the same way that roads and highways are accessible to every person with the means to travel them.

The good news, despite the occasional editorial protesting otherwise, is that both forces are finally at work.

First, the breadth of content available and tailored for broadband is growing mightily, at the same time that the costs of broadband are declining. Hollywood is now programming for broadband audiences. Educators are increasingly using broadband to teach students who can't be present in the classroom. Individuals are composing, writing, photographing, and producing for the broadband medium. Radio stations are using broadband to expand the reach of their programming to anybody, anywhere. Sports teams and leagues are going online via broadband. Electronic newsgathering organizations use broadband to deliver more than what their limited over-the-air broadcasting spectrum allows. Video gaming companies are discovering a flood of demand for online multiplayer games over broadband. Merchants are transforming online commerce from a dull world of text and static images to a multimedia shopping mall.

More reasons than ever exist for people to be compelled by the broadband experience. The network is a breeding ground for innovation in nearly every sector of the economy, and the days of signing up for broadband merely to overcome the frustration of slow-loading web pages are long gone.

At the same time, we're beginning to see the healthy fruits of a competitive market for broadband services. Prices are coming down in many places where at least two providers compete for customers. In May 2003, the U.S. telephone company Verizon announced it would reduce the cost of its entry-level 1.5 Mbps DSL service to $29.95 a month, from $34.95 (at least for customers who buy a package of services from the company). Cable television companies, too, are beginning to lower prices for some cable modem services, typically allowing customers to select from several data-rate options that feature different price points. Broadband has been growing fast—relative to other consumer media and electronics technologies—even without the contribution of intensive price competition. These recent examples of discounting are likely to propel broadband adoption rates even further.

The second big driver of adoption—availability—is no longer much of an issue, at least in most developed nations. Within the world's 20 largest economies, more than 300 million households across the world have access to broadband networks. In 15 of these nations, including South Korea, the U.S., Canada, Japan, Spain, Australia, France, Italy, Belgium, and the U.K., broadband is available to more than two-thirds of all households. Availability continues to grow by the day, as consumers demonstrate their willingness to pay for broadband connectivity.

In fact, although broadband is a young technology, in some places the market has already begun to show signs of near-saturation, or a condition in which broadband is virtually ubiquitous. The largest U.S. cable television company, Comcast Corp., has announced that 94 percent of its network facilities will have been rebuilt to accommodate broadband services by the end of 2003. Verizon says DSL will be available over 80 percent of its telephone access lines by the end of 2003.

Overall in the U.S., the federal government estimates broadband is available to nearly 80 percent of homes, and a majority of households have a choice of at least two providers. With any luck, that number will grow to three or more as interesting progress continues in wireless and, more recently, two-way satellite networks that could ignite further competition.

These dynamics are worth noting given the increasing interest among governments in fostering a wide-scale broadband conversion among their citizens. Over the last several years, advanced nations have been quick to recognize the next stage of their economic growth depends upon the emergence of broadband. South Korea has gone to the greatest lengths to foster rapid broadband deployment. With the Asian economy reeling in the late 1990s, Korean policy makers took a big gamble on broadband, investing in a nationwide fiber-and-DSL network that has since flourished, in terms at least of usage if not economic reward. Today, despite losses from its investment, South Korea is the embodiment of the wired nation.

In South Korea, broadband is available to 95 percent of all households. More than half of that nation's 15 million households are now connected to high-speed networks that allow them to attend school, watch soap operas, and play games over high-bit-rate DSL broadband networks that start at about $32 a month and top out at an impressive 40 Mbps.

Steep government subsidies to accelerate broadband leave a sour philosophical taste to many, but without question, South Korea and its world-leading broadband penetration is the envy of many a content producer, online business provider, or distance-learning educator. Among those quick to benefit from South Korea's fast-track broadband uptake are online retailers. Home shopping, the consulting firm Accenture reports, now makes up nearly nine percent of all retail sales in South Korea and could double by 2005. Also thriving with broadband is the Seoul Broadcasting System. Close to 10,000 Korean broadband users pay about 40 cents a day to watch reruns of the popular Korean soap opera "All In."

China, too, is taking up the broadband cause in a big way, and more than a few interested sociologists are watching to see how one of the world's largest but most isolated nations reacts to the infiltration of broadband connectivity. Only about one million homes within a nation of one billion people are broadband-enabled, but zealous proponents such as Edward Tian aim to change that. Tian, the chief executive officer of China Netcom Communications, is on a mission to build one of the largest and fastest broadband networks in the world. Already Tian has build hundreds of optical fiber nodes and laid cables connecting China's largest cities. In the invisible data flows of his broadband network, Tian sees the makings of an economic and social transformation in China, with implications for health care, education, and more. In an apocryphal *Wired* magazine quote, Tian says, "Enlightenment can flow through the taps like water."

Similarly heady thoughts about broadband echo elsewhere. The president of TechNet, the advocacy group led by U.S. technology executives who are anxious to sell lots of enabling gadgets for broadband, has likened universal broadband access to the feat of putting a man on the moon. Larry Babbio, the chairman of Verizon, delivered a June 2002 speech in which he said broadband "is not just about cable modems and DSL, as we tend to think of it today. It's about enriching people's lives; simplifying the work environment; and delivering information and the Internet experience to every individual's doorstep." U.S. Senator Joseph Lieberman, introducing legislation to spur wider broadband adoption, said broadband is "the ultimate economic stimulus, the next superhighway system for our next generation of leaders, our children, and grandchildren."

Rhetoric aside, it is widely agreed that broadband represents a potentially huge economic contributor. Start with the fact that the information technology sector at large already is a big part of most modern economies. The U.S. Commerce Department reports that information technology (IT) accounted for more than half of the productivity gains registered in the U.S. economy since 1995, and produced 1.2 million new jobs from 1995–2000. IT has infiltrated our work lives and our economic lives in a pervasive fashion. By now, everybody knows somebody who is employed in the IT sector.

Within this IT arena, broadband will play an increasingly prominent role. The broadband network will enhance economic activity in markets spanning communications, entertainment, education, health care, security, and overall business productivity. Economists Robert Crandall and Charles L. Jackson, writing for the Brookings Institution, estimate that universal broadband availability could produce a staggering $500 billion in gross domestic economic benefit to the U.S. by 2006. Another study by The Yankee Group, a telecommunications research and consulting company, says businesses could save $233 billion by managing more processes and activities over a broadband network.

Part of broadband's economic contribution is the building of the network itself — a massive endeavor that has already created thousands of new jobs. Yet the ripple effect is bigger still. Stephen Pociask, an economist and expert in telecommunications markets, estimates that building out a universally available U.S. broadband network would produce 237,000 direct jobs in manufacturing and construction. He also projects it would create another 974,000 jobs in broadband applications and content areas, such as new interactive media, games and entertainment, multimedia videoconferencing, and digital video broadcasting. Students of the future, take note. There could be worse career moves than a specialization in broadband-enabled applications.

Beyond creating jobs, broadband stands to leave a positive imprint on a variety of economic, life, and social conditions. The way we purchase goods is one example. In tests staged by the e-commerce retailer eBags Inc., compared with consumers who view static photos, those who watch video displays of luggage via broadband are 19 percent more likely to buy. A survey by the investment banking firm Goldman Sachs and Chicago researcher Synovate shows broadband customers shop more via the web than other online patrons—29 percent more annually, to be exact. Imagine the implications for the day—certain to come—when broadband connections finally eclipse narrowband hookups.

Broadband creates many economic ripple effects. The U.S. Office of Technology Policy, an arm of the Commerce Department, observes that broadband allows new businesses to locate wherever they choose, potentially contributing to economic growth in locales that desperately need it. In Pittsburgh, the city has turned rusting and empty steel plants into broadband-laced research centers that allow new companies to sprout, reviving blocks of fallow urban property.

The Office of Technology Policy also notes that wider broadband deployment in schools could reverse a starkly ironic condition: the fact that most kids today are steeply immersed in digital technologies everywhere in their lives except at school. As Education Secretary Rodney Paige rather eloquently puts it, "We still educate our students based on an agricultural timetable, in an industrial setting, yet tell students they live in a digital age. The problem is not that we have expected too much from technology in education—it is that we have settled for too little."

Broadband quickly is seeping into higher education and the growing field of distance-learning, which already serves more than 2.2 million U.S. college students, many of whom have daytime jobs and are too time-strapped to attend lectures in physical classrooms. Messages such as the one appearing on Tulane University's distance-learning website are now commonplace: "Regarding Internet connectivity, a broadband connection (DSL, cable) is recommended." Marsha Ham, a distance-learning program specialist at the University of Arizona, says broadband opens up the promise of the Internet for educational purposes in ways that dialup connectivity hasn't. Previously, "the bandwidth issues restricted everything that could happen," says Ham. "It's only now where the bandwidth allows you to do new things."

National security interests, too, depend mightily on broadband, which is used by strategists to survey battlegrounds, communicate with subordinates and, one hopes, limit casualties. The top military challenge facing the U.S. in its 2002 conflict in Afghanistan wasn't improved weaponry, but the need for more bandwidth to command and control the effort, said Joint Chiefs of Staff vice director Major General Charles Croom.

With broadband taking on an ever-higher profile within core economic and governmental arenas, it's likely that the U.S. and possibly other governments will establish national offices of broadband policy to assure a concerted momentum behind the broadband transformation.

Already, in many developed nations, broadband is well on the way toward an important goal—to make broadband service accessible to virtually the entire population base of nations, with technical performance standards that meet or exceed the following:

- Constant data rates of at least 10 million bits per second per home, all the time
- Bandwidth that is always on, operates as reliably as modern telephone networks, and is secure, is devoid of latency issues, and is engineered to deliver continuous, uninterrupted services at all times
- Support for a range of secure voice, data, and video services, with growing room for a continually expanding range of applications

Such an initiative, although lofty, would augment and accelerate broadband deployment for use by all citizens. It won't be cheap: An investment exceeding $1000 per household, would likely be required, especially to get to broadband ubiquity within 10 years.

The word "initiative" might make some free-market capitalists skittish, but keep in mind that a devoted intrusion by government isn't what we're talking about. Rather, a cooperative, like-minded approach among multiple parties and dependent on open-market competition can best achieve what many agree is a national imperative. Furthering the presence of broadband to a critical mass of people requires passion on the part of numerous business and public sector leaders, from innovators in delivering home health care to designers who dream up the latest addictive multiplayer video games.

National governments certainly can play a role here on many fronts. They can support investments in capital equipment and plant necessary to advance high-speed broadband, through tax incentives and economic policies that reward, or at least avoid punishing, risk taking. They can make funds available for broadband deployment in cases where private-market economics might not work. The Bush administration, for example, has proposed loaning $196 million to telecommunications companies to build high-speed broadband networks in rural towns and communities.

Governments themselves can make more use of broadband, potentially spurring demand, by using the broadband infrastructure to provide improved government services and information. (Broadband access to an instant video clip explaining an impenetrable tax form could save many a headache for U.S. taxpayers every April.) Governments can also enforce laws that protect the sanctity of intellectual property that flows over broadband conduits. In addition, they can, and should, steadfastly avoid regulations that stifle free speech or limit content available over broadband networks.

Policy decisions that foster competition within the broadband arena are also necessary. Government leaders are wrestling with many of these broadband policy questions now. In the U.S., these decisions run the gamut from figuring out how to allow broadband facilities companies to burrow through backyards to lay cable, to allocating swaths of spectrum for new wireless broadband services, to wading through the policy muck of whether to grant certain market protections to telephone companies in exchange for mandating faster data rates to the home.

Competition matters not just for obvious reasons of encouraging affordable pricing and fostering superior innovations, but for ensuring that the widest possible array of broadband services makes its way to consumers. Since the first residential broadband customers were hooked on the service in the mid-1990s, there has been a steady murmur of concern that the owners of broadband delivery facilities—the cable and DSL networks that bring us our speedy data rates—will be tempted to exert control over what applications and what content flow over their high-speed pipes.

Having invested billions of dollars in shareholder funds to build their networks, it is fair to argue that facilities owners should be able to derive whatever economic reward they can from them. However, it is important for consumers to have the ultimate arbitration here. If carrier A chooses to disallow certain content, or limit access to third-party applications, or prevent you from watching a legally provided television show of your liking over your broadband-connected PC or television set, there should be a carrier B, C, and beyond willing to permit you to do whatever it is you want to do over your broadband connection—as long as you're willing to pay for it. The likelihood is that over time, few carriers will deem it wise to limit choice.

Instead, it's likely that new pricing schemes will come into play. If you tend to use broadband applications that gobble up huge expanses of network capacity, at least relative to your more restrained neighbor, it might be perfectly reasonable for you to pay more for that particular privilege. However, facilities-based providers who attempt to put artificial walls around what can and cannot be accessed over a broadband connection should do so only at their own peril—and policy makers would be wise to ensure the most competitive market exists for multiple players in the broadband field.

In part, that means learning from past mistakes. The U.S. 1996 Tele-communications Act was a disastrous attempt to force-feed a highly intrusive national policy upon the local exchange carriers of the telephone industry. In the ensuing mountain of regulations designed to "unbundle" the raw facilities of telephony, lived the bizarre notion that it was quite proper to require local telephone companies to provide their equipment—at government-determined costs—to competitors. These competitors were then free to poach broadband customers away from the same phone companies that provided the upstarts their means of delivery in the first place. Meanwhile, cable television companies were left relatively untouched, at least from a facilities-access standpoint, and have gamely outsold DSL by more than two-to-one in the U.S. market.

The lesson here might be that the best policy is to spur genuine competition—the sort that involves real capital investment in owned-and-operated facilities—rather than to demand that an incumbent provider share its hard-earned goods with rivals, and may the better broadband mousetrap win.

Without a magic wand to wave, broadband simply needs time and room to grow, from a regulatory standpoint. It needs to inspire more inventors and thinkers to develop applications that truly dazzle. Pricing probably needs to drift downward from the prevalent $45 per month or so. Customer service could stand to improve (and it is; provisioning a fresh DSL line now takes days, not weeks. Cable modem installations are increasingly simple enough to be accomplished within 15 minutes, or by users themselves.) Primarily, broadband needs the most powerful tonic of all—positive word-of-mouth endorsement from satisfied users. Happily, all of these are present today and in good working order.

The sense among some broadband proponents is that a sort of tipping point has in fact been achieved. Larry Shapiro, the Walt Disney Internet Group executive and strategist, notes that in the U.S., broadband's achievement of 20 million subscribing households in 2003 is significant. "It's sort of the magic point in the U.S.," he says, "where you're starting to get beyond the early adopters of people who just want speed for speed's sake. You're now getting to an audience that finds some value or entertainment or utility in the experience that can be only delivered by broadband— rather than just reading their e-mail faster."

On that front, as policy makers, technology manufacturers, broadband network operators, and just about anybody else looks out over the horizon, all would agree that we've only begun to test the possibilities of the broadband network.

Many believe the next generations of broadband access networks will leapfrog our prevalent cable and DSL-based networks, which today tend to be highly asymmetrical (much faster going to the home than coming away from it) and generally don't yet achieve the 10 Mbps gold-standard (or something even higher). For example, there remain high hopes and grand visions for the deployment of high-capacity optical fiber networks that would bring directly to the home the sort of industrial-strength data performance that is normally associated with the Internet backbone, not the last-mile conduit.

Futurists believe the ultimate broadband delivery scheme could be something called a passive optical network (PON), or, in modern industry lingo, a "fiber-to-the-curb" or "fiber-to-the-home" network. PONs are usually presented to the world as supercharged broadband networks, capable of downstream rates of 600 Mbps or more, and upstream rates of 155 Mbps—speeds that dwarf today's cable and DSL access network performance, and are heralded as delivering improved security and reliability.

Maybe in the reader's lifetime the PON and its glorious capability will in fact arrive at the doorstep, complete with free installation and 10 percent off for the first six months. If that's the case, however, somebody's going to have to pay for it, and it had better be substantially superior to the trusty cable modem or incumbent DSL connection.

Fiber-to-the-curb growth projections often ignore the steadily rising customer base being cultivated by our existing access technologies, and fail to pay honest heed to the fact that displacing incumbent delivery networks isn't quite child's play. Radio, once believed doomed thanks to the onset of television, remains alive and well, for example. The onset of the PON is more likely to occur, at least in the next progression of broadband access, as an enhancement to an existing access cable or DSL network rather than a wholesale competitive substitute. It costs real money, remember, to bury fiber lines, string coax from telephone poles, and dispatch professionally trained installers to hook up subscribers, one by one and house by house.

Fiber does seem destined to creep further into the network, true, but it is anybody's guess as to how far and how fast. Even then, there's no assurance that fiber-to-the-curb schemes will be the only way to feed 100 Mbps of data to the home. A crop of inventive and persistent engineers remains hard at work right now to coax ever-greater leaps of performance from existing DSL and cable broadband access networks. Wireless networks and satellite-fed broadband remain extremely interesting and laden with potential. Plus, there's no substitute for hard, sunk cash. When contemplating the fortunes estimated to be needed to bring 100 Mbps to the average home, remember that there has been a substantial chunk of money already invested. By some estimates, for example, U.S. cable television operators have shoveled some $70 billion in capital into their physical plant over the 1997–2003 time frame, a large amount of it for the very purpose of delivering broadband data streams to the home.

Cable, DSL, PON, satellite, or something else, the time for broadband is here. Beginning more than 65 years ago, the high-speed highway and the automobile replaced the public railway networks as an economic infrastructure. Now the time has come to make another replacement. The suburbanization of the U.S., and other western nations, is complete. The support structures that both fostered and served the geographic organization of nations have peaked, and are well past their optimal effective contribution. It has gotten to the point where they're not saving time, but costing time for the average citizen.

New high-speed, time-saving systems need to be deployed—everywhere. Governments should work to foster the continuing advance of broadband, giving it the same sort of attention accorded to other economic support pillars for transportation, electric power, postal systems, communications, security, and others, reaching all citizens and contributing to an improved lifestyle. To that end, what follows is a list, randomly arrayed, of some of the things broadband allows us to do now, or will enable in the near future. Rare is the reader who won't find some affinity for one or many of the following applications:

- Child Monitoring
  - Use your broadband connection to enable a "Net-nanny" service that allows you to keep tabs on your children remotely
  - Enable a local area network intercom system that lets you coo to your baby from a remote location—for example, a hotel
  - Watch your daughter recite her third-grade class presentation while you're at the home office
- Security Management
  - Dial 911 automatically in the case of an intrusion or theft
  - Allow entry based on visual/facial identification
  - Enable an effective home-monitoring system using web cams

- Home/Family Management
    - Share access to an instant, always-available family events and scheduling calendar
    - View digital photos on the television or any web-enabled display device
    - Look up recipes on demand from a broadband-connected monitor affixed to your refrigerator
- Communications
    - Find out who is calling you on the telephone by looking at a caller-ID display on your TV screen
    - Send a voice-mail message using your e-mail outbox
    - Enjoy unified messaging—the ability to collect and interact with messages from multiple devices: your fax, e-mail, or telephone
- Gaming
    - Play against your brother upstairs—or a friend halfway across the world
    - Immerse yourself in 3-D worlds with immediate response
    - Summon games on demand, without the need for a physical disc or cartridge
- Home Systems
    - Control your heating, ventilation, and air conditioning from a distant location
    - Turn on lights and appliances before you get home
    - Keep energy consumption low when you're not there
    - Turn your sprinkler system on or off from anywhere
- Health Care
    - Converse with your doctor without driving to the office
    - Monitor and report vital signs from home
    - Allow your physician to monitor your condition via video
- Education
    - Participate in live video lectures with interactive capability
    - Summon on-demand video lectures at a schedule you determine
    - Translate lessons and lectures into the language you prefer

- Entertainment
  - Watch television from multiple devices in multiple rooms of the house
  - Enjoy television on demand, on a schedule you determine
  - Stream song lyrics to a display device as you listen
- Community
  - Send video clips to friends and relatives with ease
  - Watch and participate in local government meetings
  - Monitor traffic and travel conditions in real-time

Summary

In June of 1928, the gifted writer E.B. White wrote for *The New Yorker* magazine an article titled "Tadpoles and Telephones." As White reported, the New York Telephone Company had placed within its sidewalk window a large bowl of tadpoles, accompanied by a sign that read, "The Tadpole Reminds Us." The metaphor was that the tadpole, forced to rise to the surface of the water again and again merely to breathe, was like the businessman denied access to his own desktop telephone. Just like the tadpole, he would have to leave his desk repeatedly to conduct business. Life would be better, the company was suggesting, if more people had more telephones.

White's tadpole dispatch points out an important historical milestone about technology—a reminder, in these days of instant gratification and prolific technological bounty, that it wasn't always this way. There was a time when telephones were novelties. The New York Telephone Company was on the front end of what would become a 100-year strategy: Market new technologies and services to businesses first; then residences. A phone on every businessman's desk; a phone in every home. It took seven decades, but it happened.

The next tadpole reminder, as logical a progression as the telephone or the personal computer, is broadband. Whether it comes from telephone companies or cable companies, wireless broadcasters or satellite, broadband is on the move. More than 40 million households are connected to broadband already. Services are converging, such that the connections that deliver video to cable customers and phone services to telephone customers can be kneaded into doing far more than originally intended.

That notion of supplying telephone, video, and high-speed digital data service, in any combination, to any number of receiving devices in a home, is broadband. My hunch is that it, too, will ultimately wind its way into most of our homes, changing our daily lives, for the better. It's a lofty goal. It won't be a smooth transition. There will be hiccups, industrial metamorphosis, and heated regulatory debates. However, the result, I am convinced, will be a better place for us all to work, live, and thrive. Broadband will save massive amounts of energy. It will protect our planet by reducing our consumption of fossil fuels and our habit of spilling out pollutants. Broadband will allow us to replace the industrial-age behavior of commuting to physical locations in order to accomplish things.

Broadband is the enabling agent for something important: the third revolution in mankind. We have progressed from an agriculture age to an industrial age. The information age, long ago promised, is finally here, thanks to broadband.

INDEX

subscribers
AOL customers, 19
by country (table), 6–8
in developing nations, 66
in South Korea, 9
RealNetworks subscriptions, 112
worldwide statistics, 65
**suggested data rates for broadband
network tasks, 11–12**

T

T1 lines, 29
**tables, broadband subscribers by
country, 6–8**
**TCP/IP (Transmission Control
Protocol/Internet Protocol), 26**
TechNet advocacy groups, 68–69
Telecommunications Act of 1996, 31–34
telephony
networks, 28
VoIP, 122
Tele-TV, 30
**television, viewing habits of broad-
band users, 80**
teleworking, 97
activities of teleworkers, 100
advantages of, 101–102
environmental benefits, 103
productivity, 103
barriers to overcome, 101
defining, 97
feasibility of, 99
in Finland, 97
in Japan, 97
ITAC, 97
popularity of, 101
residential broadband users, 99

Tian, Edward, 127
top providers of broadband, 63
tracking availability of broadband, 69
two-way cable architecture, 40

U

U.S. 1996 Telecommunications Act, 131
unused backbone data capacity, 70
user-generated content, 114–116

V

video
impact on e-commerce, 116
impact on DSL development, 30
RealNetworks subscription services, 112
user-generated content, 115–116
video games, 120
VoIP, 122
Vonage, 122

W–Z

Wadsworth, Steve, 121
Whitman, Meg, 116
**widespread availability of broadband
as national imperative, 69**
Wi-Fi, 57, 61
wireless networks
Bluetooth, 60
broadband, 57–58
IrDA, 60